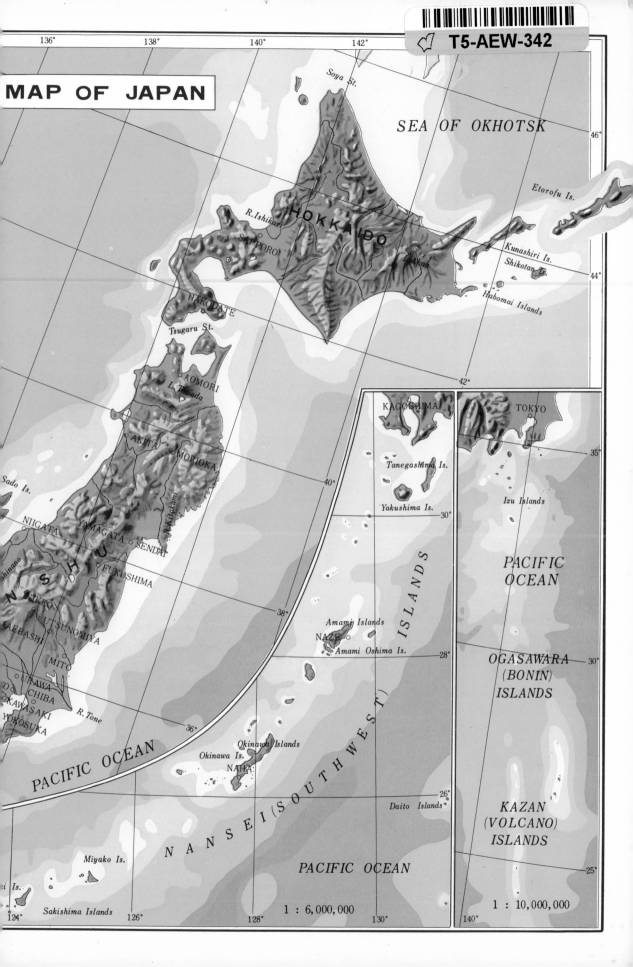

MAP OF JAPAN

SEA OF OKHOTSK

HOKKAIDO

Soya St.

R.Ishikari

SAPPORO

Etorofu Is.

Kunashiri Is.

Shikotan Is.

Habomai Islands

HAKODATE

Tsugaru St.

AOMORI

L. Towada

AKITA

MORIOKA

Sado Is.

NIIGATA

YAMAGATA

SENDAI

R.Kitakami

FUKUSHIMA

NIKKO

UTSUNOMIYA

MAEBASHI

MITO

CHIBA

KAWASAKI

YOKOSUKA

R. Tone

Shinano

PACIFIC OCEAN

KAGOSHIMA

TOKYO

Tanegashima Is.

Yakushima Is.

Izu Islands

PACIFIC OCEAN

Amami Islands

NAZE

Amami Oshima Is.

OGASAWARA
(BONIN)
ISLANDS

ISLANDS

NANSEI(SOUTHWEST)

Okinawa Islands

Okinawa Is.

NAHA

Daito Islands

KAZAN
(VOLCANO)
ISLANDS

PACIFIC OCEAN

Miyako Is.

Sakishima Islands

1 : 6,000,000

1 : 10,000,000

THE JAPAN OF TODAY

Ministry of Foreign Affairs, Japan
1970

THE JAPAN OF TODAY

CONTENTS

INTRODUCTION

Japan has been called the world's most rapidly changing society. At the same time, Japan rests upon traditions reaching back into the mists of time. History and tradition, far from imposing barriers to change, have actually stimulated change in Japan in a manner perhaps unknown in other nations of the world.

Throughout their long history, the Japanese people have shown a unique aptitude for assimilating and adapting new ideas to their particular cultural milieu. This aptitude stems from the history and geography of Japan which have created an unusually homogeneous people. Over the centuries, they developed institutions, customs and characteristics that have given them a strong sense of national identity and common purpose.

The strength and stability derived from these features of the national life helped Japan undergo two major transformations in the last one hundred years, first in the late 19th century when it threw off a stagnant feudal system to embark upon the road to modernization, and again in the mid-20th century when it turned away from the tragic experience of World War II to create a new society dedicated to peaceful cooperation and the democratic way of life. While these two periods wrought almost revolutionary change in both the political and social structure, this was accomplished without discarding traditional roots or impairing social continuity.

One measure of this transformation is the

Rocky coastline of southern Izu Peninsula.

high level of economic growth attained during the last quarter of a century in which Japan has made itself into one of the world's leading industrial nations. In terms of a longer passage of time, Japan has transformed itself from an agricultural society content with minimum standards of living a mere one hundred years ago into an industrial society beginning to enjoy the standards associated with the mass consumption age.

A second measure of this change can be found in the gradual internationalization of almost all aspects of the national life. Long limited in their contacts with the outside world, first by the accident of island geography, then by self-imposed isolation for two and a half centuries, and finally in the present century by war and occupation, the Japanese are now seeking their proper role within the framework of international cooperation. Japan today belongs to all major world forums, actively pursues a diplomacy for peace and is contributing to greater mutual understanding as an active member of the community of nations.

In the new decade of the seventies, change will still characterize Japan's development as the people seek solutions to newly arising problems in the political, economic and social fields and as the nation accepts growing responsibilities in the international arena. Buttressed by their long history and by a fundamental sense of order and discipline, the Japanese people approach these challenges as their new tasks for the future and are determined to participate positively in the search for peace and justice in cooperation with all peoples who share like ideals.

GEOGRAPHY

Area

Japan consists of four main islands—Hokkaido, Honshu, Shikoku and Kyushu—in addition to a number of island chains and thousands of smaller islands and islets. The archipelago, lying off the eastern coast of the Asian continent, stretches in an arc, 3,800 kilometers long. It covers an area of 377,384 square kilometers (145,670 square miles).

Area of Main Islands (km²)

Hokkaido	78,513
Honshu	230,722
Shikoku	18,772
Kyushu	41,993

Japan's total land area is about one-twenty-fifth that of the United States, one-ninth that of India, and one-and-a-half times as big as that of the United Kingdom. In terms of world land area, Japan occupies less than 0.3 per cent.

Climate

The islands of Japan lie in the temperate zone and at the northeastern end of the monsoon area which reaches as far as India from Japan through Korea, China and Southeast Asia. The climate is generally mild, although it varies considerably from place to place, largely due to the continental air currents from the northwest, dominating the winter weather, and the Oceanic air currents from the southeast in the summer months.

The four seasons are clearly distinct. Summer, which is warm and humid, begins around the middle of July following a rainy season which usually lasts for about a month.

Except in northern Japan, the winter is mild with many sunny days. The spring and autumn are the best seasons of the year with balmy days and bright sunshine, although September brings typhoons which may strike inland with their torrential rains and violent winds.

Rainfall is abundant, ranging from 1,000 mm to 2,500 mm (40 to 100 inches) a year. Snow is heavy in the northern parts of the country and in the interior mountainous regions in winter, providing superb sites for winter sports. Tokyo, the capital city, on the other hand, enjoys a relatively mild winter with low humidity and an occasional snowfall in contrast to the high temperatures and humidity of the summer months.

Japan also enjoys many hours of sunshine throughout the year with Tokyo having 2,019 sunlight hours per year on the average.

The combination of plentiful rainfall and a temperate climate produces rich forests and a luxurious vegetation which appear to cover the entire countryside.

Topography

These climatic advantages are offset in a sense by the very complex topography. The Japanese islands are part of the "Circum-Pacific Orogenic Zone" which runs from Southeast Asia through Japan to the Aleutian Islands and Alaska in the United States. While this has given Japan a long and rocky coastline with many small but excellent harbors, it has also created a large number of mountainous areas with numerous valleys, swift-flowing rivers and clear-water lakes. In fact, mountains account for about 80 per cent of Japan's total land area. More than 580 of these mountains are over 2,000 meters high and the highest is Mt. Fuji, whose perfect cone rises some 3,776 meters (12,385 feet).

Mt. Fuji is a dormant volcano, its last eruption being in 1707. In all, Japan has 196 volcanoes, of which 30 are still active. These provide the country with one of its most pleasant amenities—mineral hot springs which are tapped more for recreational than for medical purposes. These springs feed numerous hot-spring resorts which cater to millions of Japanese holidaymakers in search of rest and relaxation.

This volcanic activity also indicates the relatively "young age" of the Japanese islands, geologically, in the sense that the land structure is still being formed. This gives rise to frequent earth tremors, which go unnoticed by the average citizen, and an occasional earthquake.

In the overall picture, however, Japan's topography provides the land with some beautiful and at times dramatic scenery: snowfed mountain lakes, rocky gorges and turbulent rivers, rugged peaks and graceful waterfalls. These are a constant source of inspiration and pleasure to the Japanese and foreign visitors alike.

Hamana-ko Bridge and Service Area on the Tomei (Tokyo-Nagoya) Expressway in Shizuoka Prefecture.▶

HISTORY

The experts disagree about the origins of the Japanese race, but archaeologists have established that its early inhabitants included immigrants from various parts of East Asia and the South Pacific islands.

The ancestors of the Japanese people are generally believed to be an ethnic group, now known as the Yamato Race, which gradually asserted its supremacy over other warring tribes and clans during the first three or four centuries A. D. The Yamato leaders are generally accepted as the ancestors of the Japanese Imperial Family.

By the end of the 4th century A.D., contact was established between Japan and the kingdoms on the Korean Peninsula. Through Korea, industrial arts such as weaving, metal work, tanning and shipbuilding, which had been highly developed in China under the Han Dynasty, were introduced into the country. During these early years, Korea and China were the sources from which Japan derived its crafts, arts and learning that formed the foundations on which its own culture was gradually built.

The written form of Chinese, which uses ideographs or characters, was adopted, and through this medium the Japanese learned the rudiments of medicine, the secrets of the calendar and astronomy, and Confucianism. Buddhism was also introduced into Japan in 538 from India through China and Korea. The Chinese system of government provided a pattern on which Japan's rulers built their own system.

The country's first permanent capital was established in Nara at the beginning of the 8th century. For more than 70 years, from 710 to 784, Japan's Imperial Family resided there and gradually extended its authority across the country. Until then, the capital had been moved each time the Emperor died.

A new capital was built in 794 in Kyoto. It was modeled on the Chinese capital of the time and remained the seat of the Emperor for nearly 1,000 years.

◄ *Horyuji Temple in Nara, founded in 607, includes the world's oldest wooden buildings.*

The transfer of the capital to Kyoto marked the beginning of the Heian Period, which continued until 1192. This was one of the great periods of artistic development. Contacts with China were interrupted toward the end of the 9th century, and Japan's civilization began to take on its own special characteristics and forms.

This was a process of assimiliation and adaptation by which what had been introduced from outside gradually assumed an essentially Japanese style. The most typical instance of this process was the development during the Heian Period of a native Japanese script. The complexity of Chinese ideographs led writers and priests to work out two sets of syllabaries based upon Chinese forms. By the middle of the Heian Period, these relatively simple letters, or *kana*, as they are called, had been perfected and brought into fairly wide use, opening the way for a literature of a pure Japanese style which was to flourish in place of that in the imported Chinese idiom.

Life in the capital was marked by great elegance and refinement. While the court gave itself up to the pursuit of the arts and social pleasures, its authority over the martial clans in the provinces became increasingly uncertain. Effective control of the realms gradually passed out of its hands and became the prize for which two rival military families, the Minamotos and Tairas, both of which traced their descent from previous Emperors, engaged in one of the most celebrated and hard-fought struggles in Japan's turbulent middle ages. The Minamotos finally prevailed, annihilating the rival Taira clan in the epic Battle of Dannoura in the Inland Sea in 1185.

Feudal Age

The victory of the Minamotos marked the virtual eclipse of the Imperial Throne as the source of effective political power and the beginning of seven centuries of feudal rule under a succession of *Shogun*, or military rulers.

In 1192, Yoritomo, head of the victorious Minamoto family, established the Shogunate, or military government, at Kamakura, near what is today Tokyo, and assumed all administrative powers that had previously been held by the Emperors in Kyoto. In a reaction against what it considered the decadence of Kyoto in its devotion to the arts of peace, the Shogunate in Kamakura encouraged austerity and the pursuit of the martial arts and disciplines required to restore effective control through the land, especially over restive clans in the remoter provinces. While the preceding Heian Period was one in which the arts flourished, the Kamakura Period, as the age of Yoritomo's Shogunate is called, was an era in which *Bushido*—the way of the Samurai, or Japanese chivalry—prevailed.

In 1213, power was transferred from the Minamotos to the Hojos, the family of Yoritomo's wife, who maintained the military government in Kamakura until 1333. During this period, the Mongolians twice attacked northern Kyushu, once in 1274 and again in 1281. Despite inferior arms, Japanese warriors successfully held the field and prevented the invaders from penetrating into the interior. Following the destruction of most of their fleet by typhoons which struck on both attempted invasions, the Mongolian force withdrew from Japan.

A short-lived restoration of Imperial rule, from 1333 to 1338, was followed by a new military government established by the Ashikagas at Muromachi in Kyoto.

The Muromachi Period continued for more than two centuries, from 1338 to 1573. Once again the pendulum swung back, from the Spartan disciplines of the Kamakura Period to a way of life in which the austere disciplines of *Bushido* chivalry found expression in aesthetic and religious activities and set their mark indelibly for all ages on the country's arts, whose chief characteristic even today is a classic sense of restraint and simplicity.

After two centuries of rule, the Shogunate in Muromachi was confronted by a growing challenge to its authority from rival clans in other parts of the country. Towards the end of the 16th century, Japan was torn by civil wars as provincial lords battled for supremacy. Order was finally restored by the great general, Hideyoshi Toyotomi, in 1590. His work of pacifying and uniting the country was consolidated by Ieyasu Tokugawa, founder of the Tokugawa Shogunate.

It was during this transition period of civil wars (1573-1603) that many of Japan's most famous castles were built.

Having established himself as effective ruler of all Japan, Ieyasu founded his Shogunate in Edo, as Tokyo was then known, in 1603. This was a major turning point in Japanese history. Ieyasu created the mold in which almost every facet of the nation's life, particularly its political and social institutions, was cast for the next 265 years.

As one means to preserve the integrity of the social and political structure which Ieyasu erected, the Tokugawa Shogunate took the drastic step of virtually closing Japan's doors to the outside world in 1639. The first Westerners had reached the shores of Japan in the previous century during the Muromachi Period. Portuguese traders landed on a small island in southwestern Japan in 1543, introducing firearms into the country. They were followed in the next few years by Jesuit missionaries, led by St. Francis Xavier, and groups of Spaniards. Dutch and British traders also established themselves on Japanese soil.

The influx of Europeans had a profound influence on Japan. The missionaries made numerous converts, particularly in southern Japan. The Shogunate realized that Christianity could be potentially as explosive a power as that of the firearms that accompanied them. Christianity was eventually proscribed, and the Shogunate barred entry to all foreigners, except a handful of Dutch and Chinese traders, who were confined to the small island of Dejima at Nagasaki. For two-and-a-half centuries, this tiny settlement was the only point of contact between Japan and the outside world. It was through this small door that Japanese scholars were able to acquire a basic knowledge of Western medicine and other sciences during the country's long period of isolation.

Himeji Castle, built in 1608, is representative of the splendor of feudal Japan. Its pure white walls have given rise to the name "White Heron Castle." ▶

Restoration of Imperial Rule

Japan came under increasing pressure around the end of the 18th and the beginning of the 19th century to open up its shores to the outside world. At home, the rigid social and political structure created by Ieyasu was beginning to feel the stresses caused by the advancing times.

In 1853 Commodore Matthew C. Perry of the United States entered Tokyo Bay with a squadron of four ships. He returned the following year and succeeded in persuading the Japanese to conclude a treaty of amity with his country. This was followed by the conclusion of similar treaties with Russia, Great Britain and the Netherlands in the same year, thus opening Japan once more to foreign intercourse. These treaties were changed four years later to treaties of commerce, and a similar treaty was concluded with France.

The impact of these events increased the pressure of the social and political currents that were undermining the foundations of the feudal structure. There was great turmoil for about a decade, until the feudal system of the Tokugawa Shogunate collapsed in 1867 and full sovereignty was restored to the Emperor in the Meiji Restoration in 1868.

Modern Period

The Meiji Era (1868-1912) represents one of the most remarkable periods in the history of the world. Under Emperor Meiji, the country set out to achieve in only a few decades what had taken centuries to develop in the West—the creation of a modern nation, with modern industries, modern political institutions and a modern pattern of society.

In the first year of his reign, Emperor Meiji transferred the Imperial capital from Kyoto to Edo, the seat of the former feudal government. The city was renamed Tokyo, meaning the Eastern Capital.

◀*Mt. Fuji as viewed from the Tomei Expressway.*

A Constitution was promulgated, establishing a constitutional monarchy. The old classes into which society had been divided during the feudal age were abolished. The whole country threw itself with energy and enthusiasm into the study and adoption of modern Western civilization.

The Meiji Restoration was like the bursting of a dam behind which had accumulated the energies and forces of centuries. The surge and ferment caused by the sudden release of these energies made themselves felt overseas. Before the 19th century ended, the country became involved in the Sino-Japanese War of 1894-95, and ten years later, in 1904-05, in the Russo-Japanese War. Japan emerged victorious from both, and mainly as a result of these wars regained South Sakhalin, which it had ceded to Russia in 1875 in exchange for the Kurile Islands, and acquired Formosa and Korea and special interests in Manchuria.

Emperor Meiji, whose enlightened and imaginative rule had helped to guide the nation through the dynamic decades of transformation, died in 1912, before the outbreak of World War I.

By the end of World War I, which Japan entered under the provisions of the Anglo-Japanese Alliance of 1902, Japan was recognized as one of the world's great powers. Emperor Taisho, who succeeded Emperor Meiji, was in turn succeeded by the present Emperor, His Majesty Hirohito, in 1926, and the present era, named Showa, began.

This era opened in an atmosphere of promise. The nation's industries were continuing to grow. Its political life seemed soundly rooted in parliamentary government. New factors, however, began to have a disturbing influence. The world-wide depression unsettled the nation's economic life. Public confidence in the political parties waned after the exposure of a number of scandals. The situation was exploited by extremists, and the military clique seized the opportunity offered them by the confusion of the times. The influence of the political parties steadily declined. After the outbreak of the China Incident in 1937, they were forced to unite on a single platform of co-operation in the war effort. They were finally dissolved, and in their place was erected a united national party. With the Diet's functions reduced to little more than those of a rubber-stamp, there could be no parliamentary obstruction to the tide of events that finally led to the outbreak of the Pacific War in 1941.

Finally, in August 1945, an exhausted and battle-weary nation accepted the surrender terms of the Allied Powers and by Imperial Edict the people laid down their arms.

Seven years later, in September 1951, Japan signed the Peace Treaty at San Francisco with 48 nations and regained its sovereign independence in April 1952 when the Treaty came into effect. Japan once again took its place as a member of the community of nations, ending a period of change hardly less revolutionary than that in the previous century under Emperor Meiji.

Within about one year following the signing of the Treaty, Japan had joined all the specialized agencies of the United Nations and in December 1956 was admitted to full membership as the 80th member state of the world body.

This acceptance in the world community seemed to signal a revitalization of Japan and the following decade was characterized by a degree of economic growth and development perhaps unprecedented in the history of any nation.

The success of this process of growth and development received recognition when, in October 1964, Tokyo was the host city for the 18th Olympic Games. The thousands of visitors from abroad found an impressive set of modern sports facilities specially constructed for the Games, as well as a pace of modernization perhaps unequalled elsewhere as symbolized by the world's first super-express rail service on the New Tokaido Line, a rapidly expanding network of urban expressways and an energetic building program, public and private, which was literally transforming the face of the nation's cities.

World attention again focused on Japan when in March 1970, the Japan World Exposition was formally opened in the Senri Hills outside Osaka. The first world exposition ever to be held in Asia, it brought together 77 nations of the world, the largest assemblage in the 120-year long history of the event. In terms of Japan, EXPO'70 was a culmination of the persistent efforts of the 1960's and an embodiment of its hopes for "Progress and Harmony for Mankind" in the decade of the seventies.

EXPO' 70: overall view of the exhibition site (above) and the Symbol Zone with the Tower of the Sun (below).▶

GOVERNMENT

CONSTITUTION AND EMPEROR

In the new Constitution, which was promulgated on November 3, 1946, and came into effect on May 3 the following year, the Japanese people pledge to uphold the high ideals of peace and democratic order. The Preamble of the Constitution states:

> "We, the Japanese people, desire peace for all time... We desire to occupy an honored place in an international society striving for the preservation of peace, and the banishment of tyranny and slavery, oppression and intolerance for all time from the earth."

The new Constitution differs in many important respects from the Meiji Constitution of 1889. Some of its key provisions are:

The Emperor is the symbol of the State and of the unity of the people. Sovereign power now rests with the people.

Japan renounces war as a sovereign right. It also renounces the threat or the use of force as means of settling disputes with

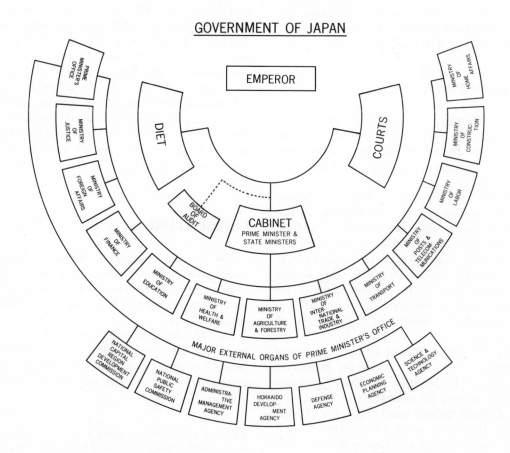

GOVERNMENT OF JAPAN

The National Diet building containing the two Houses of Parliament.

other nations.

Fundamental human rights are guaranteed as eternal and inviolable rights.

The former House of Peers is replaced by the House of Councillors, whose members, like those of the lower House of Representatives, are elected as representatives of all the people. The House of Representatives has pre-eminence over the House of Councillors.

Executive power is vested in the Cabinet, which is collectively responsible to the Diet.

Local self-government is established on an extensive scale.

The Emperor has no powers related to government. He performs only those acts that are stipulated in the Constitution. Thus, for example, he appoints the Prime Minister and the Chief Justice of the Supreme Court. The Prime Minister, however, is first designated by the Diet and the Chief Justice by the Cabinet. The Emperor also performs such acts on behalf of the people as promulgating laws and treaties, convoking the Diet and awarding honors, with the advice and approval of the Cabinet.

Imperial Family

His Majesty the Emperor of Japan, Hirohito, was born in Tokyo on April 29, 1901. He studied at the Peers' School and later at an institute specially established for his education.

As Crown Prince, he traveled in Europe for six months in 1921 and became Prince Regent shortly after his return. In 1924, he married Princess Kuni, now Empress Nagako. He succeeded to the throne in 1926. Emperor Hirohito is noted for his studies in marine biology. He devotes much of his leisure time to research in this field and has published a number of books based on his studies.

His Imperial Highness, Crown Prince Akihito, was born in Tokyo on December 23, 1933. In addition to studying under private tutors, he attended the Gakushuin Boys' High School until 1952 and Gakushuin University until 1956. He married Her Imperial Highness Crown Princess Michiko in April 1959. They have two sons and one daughter, Prince Naruhito, born

in February 1960, Prince Fumihito, born in November 1965, and Princess Sayako, born in April 1969.

The Crown Prince has traveled abroad seven times. In 1953, he attended the coronation of Her Majesty Queen Elizabeth II in London and then visited 14 countries in Western Europe and North America. In 1960, with the Crown Princess, he visited the United States and later India, Nepal, Iran and Ethiopia. In 1962, they went to Pakistan and Indonesia early in the year and later to the Philippines in November. In 1964, they went to Mexico and Thailand, and in 1967 to Argentina, Brazil and Peru.

Their most recent tour, in 1970, was to Malaysia and Singapore.

The Emperor's youngest son is His Imperial Highness Prince Hitachi. He married Her Imperial Highness Princess Hanako in September 1964. The young couple undertook a 52-day goodwill tour of Europe in October and November 1965, visiting nine countries. In 1968, they attended the centennial of Japanese emigration in Hawaii, and two years later in 1970 attended the wedding ceremonies of the Crown Prince of Nepal on behalf of His Majesty the Emperor.

With the abolition of the peerage after the war, only members of the Imperial Family retain princely titles. The daughters of the Emperor, who are all married, no longer retain their Imperial titles after marriage.

LEGISLATURE

The Diet is the highest organ of State power and the sole law-making body. It consists of the House of Representatives with 491 seats and the House of Councillors with 252 seats.

The Members of the House of Representatives are elected for a term of four years, but this term may be terminated before the expiry of the four years if the

The Imperial Palace, completed in 1968: the Seiden or State Hall facing the Central Courtyard (above) and the Minami-Damari (South Entrance Hall) for State Guests arriving on formal call.▶

House is dissolved. Members are elected from 123 constituencies and Okinawa, which, with one exception, are multi-member constituencies, returning from three to five elected members, depending on the size of the constituency and the density of population.

Members of the House of Councillors are elected for a term of six years. Half of its members are elected every three years. One hundred members are elected from what is called the National Constituency, which means that they are elected by voters throughout the country. The remaining 152 members are elected in 46 prefectural constituencies and Okinawa.

Japan has universal adult suffrage. All men and women of the age of 20 and above are eligible to vote in all elections.

Political Parties

Besides the ruling Liberal-Democratic Party, there are at present three major opposition parties: the Socialist Party, the Komei Party and the Democratic Socialist Party.

The Liberal-Democratic Party is Japan's only conservative political grouping and is at present the ruling party. Its policy aims are (1) to create a democratic order in Japan with higher living standards by reforming existing institutions in line with the basic principles of democracy; (2) to strive for improved international relations on the basis of universal justice, peace and freedom, and to build up a self-supporting and independent Japan; and (3) to ensure economic and social stability by carrying out properly formulated plans consistent with individual initiative and free enterprise, and to serve the public interest.

The primary aim of the Socialist Party is to create a socialist society in Japan through a peaceful revolution. It opposes the Treaty of Mutual Cooperation and Security (Security Treaty) between Japan and the United States of America and urges the withdrawal of U.S. military forces from

Japan. In foreign affairs, it urges a neutralist policy, with Japan's security and peace in East Asia maintained through a treaty embracing Japan, the United States, the Soviet Union and Mainland China.

The Komei Party was formed in November 1964, originally as the political arm of the "Soka Gakkai," a religious group of the Nichiren Sect of Buddhism. Participating in its first General Election in January 1967, the party succeeded in having 25 of its candidates elected to the Lower House. The aims of the party's policies include creating a welfare state based upon respect for humanity and human socialism and establishing a clean parliamentary and democratic system of government. It calls for an independent foreign policy and advocates a step-by-step dissolution of the U.S.-Japan Security Treaty in line with a strengthening of the United Nations' security functions.

The Democratic Socialist Party was formed in January 1960 by a group that broke away from the Socialist Party the previous year. It stands against extreme ideologies and is dedicated to the creation of a socialist society through democratic processes. Its policies include the achieving of full employment, a consolidated social welfare system and the raising of living standards among those in the lower income brackets. In foreign affairs, it advocates an independent policy without leaning towards any particular foreign country.

Political Party Composition of the Japanese Diet as of January 15, 1971

	House of Representatives	House of Councillors
Liberal-Democratic Party	303	136
Socialist Party	91	63
Komei Party	47	24
Democratic Socialist Party	32	9
Communist Party	14	7
Ni-in Club	—	5
Independents	3	1
Vacancies	1	7
Total	491	252

NB: Under the Diet Law, a Diet member cannot present a proposal unless supported by more than 20 members of the lower House or 10 members of the upper House.

◀ *Their Majesties the Emperor and Empress (above).*
The Imperial Family on New Year's Day, 1971 (below).

EXECUTIVE

Executive power is vested in the Cabinet, which consists of the Prime Minister and not more than 18 State Ministers and is collectively responsible to the Diet.

The Prime Minister is designated by the Diet and must himself be a member of the Diet. He has the power to appoint and dismiss the Ministers of State, all of whom must be civilians and a majority of whom must be members of the Diet.

If the House of Representatives passes a resolution of non-confidence or refuses to pass a vote of confidence in the Government, the Cabinet must resign, unless the House of Representatives is dissolved within ten days.

There are 12 ministries and 5 agencies in addition to the Prime Minister's Office, and there were in 1969 a total of 1,391,000 government employees, including 258,000 uniformed personnel of the Self-Defense Forces.

In addition to these, there is the Board of Audit, an independent constitutional body, which is responsible for the annual auditing of the accounts of the State.

For the purpose of local administration, Japan is divided into 46 prefectures, including the Metropolis of Tokyo. Local administration is conducted at the levels of prefectural, city, town and village governments, each with their respective assemblies.

The prefectural governors and city, town and village mayors, as well as the members of the local assemblies, are elected by the registered voters within the district concerned. In 1969, local goverments had a total of 2,400,000 employees, including 772,000 teachers and 166,000 policemen.

JUDICIARY

The Judiciary is completely independent of the executive and legislative branches of government.

The judiciary system consists of the Supreme Court, eight high courts, a district court in each of the prefectures, with the exception of Hokkaido which has four, and a number of summary courts. In addition, there are many family courts to adjudicate domestic complaints.

The Supreme Court is composed of a Chief Justice and 14 other Justices. The Chief Justice is appointed by the Emperor upon designation by the Cabinet, while the

other 14 Justices are appointed by the Cabinet.

The lower court judges are appointed by the Cabinet from a list of persons nominated by the Supreme Court. All lower court judges are appointed for ten years, although there is no restriction on their being re-appointed.

All judges are independent in the exercise of their conscience and are bound only by the Constitution and the laws enacted thereunder. No judge can be removed except by public impeachment unless judicially declared mentally or physically incompetent to perform his official duties. Every judge must retire at an age set by law.

The appointment of the Justices of the Supreme Court is subject to review in a national referendum, first at the time of the general election following their appointment and then at the general election following the lapse of ten-year periods. In addition, impeachment may be ordered by a Court of Impeachment, which consists of members of the House of Representatives and the House of Councillors. The Supreme Court is the court of last resort in determining questions of constitutionality of any law, order, regulation or official act.

Trials must be conducted and judgment declared publicly, unless a court unanimously determines publicity to be dangerous to public order or morals. However, trials of political offenses, offenses involving the press or cases relating to the rights of the people as guaranteed in the Constitution must always be conducted publicly.

FOREIGN RELATIONS

The basic objectives of Japanese diplomacy are to secure world peace and to carry out in a positive manner the nation's international responsibilities, which are rapidly increasing with the growth of its national strength, in the cause of easing tensions and forming an orderly climate for world peace.

To be more specific, they call for efforts

The Emperor formally opening a session of the Diet with his Address from the Throne.▶

to:

—Further enhance friendly relations and mutual understanding with other countries;

—Contribute to the economic and social development of the developing nations;

—Strive for the strengthening of the United Nations and for disarmament; and

—Further promote international interchange.

After the end of World War II, Japan made a renewed start as a peace-loving democratic nation. The people of Japan, having experienced the deep misery of war, particularly the atomic bombing of Hiroshima and Nagasaki, fervently desire everlasting peace.

The Constitution of 1946 declares that the Japanese people, who "forever renounce war as a means of settling international disputes," aspire to achieve an abiding world peace and are determined to strive toward that goal.

This ideal of the Japanese people is expressed in the nation's diplomacy for peace which recognizes the reality that Japan is extremely vulnerable from the security standpoint because it consists of a small strip of narrow but densely populated land. Furthermore, since Japan is an island nation lacking in natural resources and dependent on trade for its existence, any international dispute, even if it occurs in a remote corner of the world, could adversely affect its peace and prosperity.

In line with this diplomacy for peace, Japan is undertaking greater efforts to attain its security and prosperity through international cooperation, fully prepared to assume its growing international responsibilities commensurable with its national strength. This goal is sought on two levels: bilateral relations with other free nations having similar political systems and with nations of different political systems on the basis of mutual respect for each other's stand, and multilateral activities in international organizations and agencies devoted to promoting

◀ *Two international meetings in Tokyo for economic cooperation: Conference on Agricultural Development in Southeast Asia (above) and Ministerial Conference for the Economic Development of Southeast Asia (below).*

and contributing to world peace in many areas of human endeavor. All Japan's efforts are conducted within the framework of its ideals as a peace-loving nation, but without losing sight of the realities of the modern world.

Relationship with the United States

Japan and the United States have a close and deep relationship covering almost all aspects of their national lives and recognize the vital importance of maintaining these close ties of friendly cooperation. With the agreement reached between Prime Minister Sato and President Nixon in November 1969 to return Okinawa to Japan in 1972, the so-called "postwar period" in Japanese-American relations ended and a new age of partnership has opened between the two countries.

Located as it is in the Far East where the situation remains still fluid and uncertain, Japan has to seek the best means by which to ensure its own security. Therefore, Japan, while endeavoring to build up its self-defense capabilities within the constitutional limitation, has been following a policy of supplementing its defense effort with a mutual security system with the United States under the terms of the Japan-U.S. Treaty of Mutual Cooperation and Security.

This formula, which has been contributing not only to Japan's security but also to the maintenance of peace in the Far East, will be firmly maintained as the basis for the nation's security policy in the future.

Relationship with the Soviet Union

In October 1956, Japan and the Soviet Union signed a Joint Declaration terminating the state of war between the two countries and re-establishing diplomatic relations.

Since then, friendly cooperative relations have developed gradually but steadily between the two countries in various fields, such as trade, aviation and cultural interchange, and these relations are expanding year after year.

However, no peace treaty has yet been concluded between the two countries since territorial issues remain unsolved.

The China Problem

Japan concluded a peace treaty with the Republic of China in April 1952 and follows a policy of maintaining a friendly and cooperative relationship with this neighboring country.

At the same time, it is an undeniable fact that the Peking Government exists on the Chinese mainland and is governing a huge population of close to 800 million people. Further, Japan has had a close relationship with the Chinese mainland over the centuries.

Therefore, under its policy of promoting friendship as far as possible even with nations having different political systems, Japan intends to promote relations with the Peking Government on the basis of mutual understanding and respect while hoping that the Peking Government, for its part, will come to take a more cooperative and constructive attitude in its foreign relations.

The Problem of Indochina

As for the Indochina Peninsula, Japan earnestly hopes that peace will be restored in that part of Asia at the earliest possible date. Pending the realization of peace, Japan is providing assistance for the stabilization of the people's livelihood, and once peace is achieved, Japan is determined to offer as much aid as possible in cooperation with other nations in the interests of postwar reconstruction and the improvement of the people's living standards.

Regional Cooperation in Asia

In carrying out its responsibilities as an advanced industrial nation dedicated to the cause of peace, Japan recognizes its essential role in the Asian region with which it has close relations, geographically, historically and culturally. Since 1953, Japan has been a member of the United Nations Economic Commission for Asia and the Far East (ECAFE). In recent years, the spirit of self-help and a sense of regional cooperation have been mounting among the Asian countries. In order to promote and strengthen this atmosphere, Japan sponsored the first Ministerial Conference for the Economic Development of Southeast Asia in 1966, and made a significant contribution to the establishment of the Asian Development Bank in the same year. Furthermore, Japan has been an active member, from the beginning, of the Asian and Pacific Council (ASPAC), an organization for promoting constructive cooperation in the cause of regional peace and development, and was host to its ministerial session in June 1969.

Strengthening the U.N. and Seeking Disarmament

Since its entry into the United Nations in 1956, Japan has been cooperating to the fullest extent possible in the various activities of the world body as well as all the Specialized Agencies. Japan was twice elected a non-permanent member of the Security Council for 1958-1959 and for 1966-1967. In addition, it has been elected three times to a seat on the Economic and Social Council in 1960-1962, 1963-1965, and 1968-1970.

In order to further strengthen the U.N.'s peace-keeping functions, Japan has proposed a review of the Charter's provisions regarding the composition and voting methods of the Security Council, the powers of the General Assembly, the role of the Trusteeship Council, as well as those regarding "former enemy states."

Since its admission to the Geneva Disarmament Committee in July 1969, Japan has been contributing to the achievement of disarmament measures such as the banning of underground nuclear weapons tests, the prohibition of emplacing weapons of mass destruction on the sea-bed, and the outlawing of chemical and biological weapons. Japan signed the Nuclear Non-Proliferation Treaty in February 1970 and ratified the Geneva

In the United Nations: Japan's Foreign Minister addressing the 24th Session of the General Assembly (above); Japan's Permanent Representative presiding over a session of the Security Council.▶

Protocol which prohibits the use of poisonous gases and bacteriological weapons in May 1970.

North-South Problem

Japan fully realizes that the developing nations of the world must achieve economic and social development for their own political and social stability and ultimately for the cause of world peace.

However, the economic gap between the developed and the developing nations, far from being narrowed, is in fact tending to widen in recent years. Japan recognizes the necessity for making greater efforts, along with other developed nations, in seeking a solution to this gap and, therefore, intends to strive to achieve the target of one per cent of its gross national product as the total amount devoted to aid by 1975. At the same time, Japan is prepared to relax the terms of its aid, expand technical co-operation and step up private investments abroad, while positively approaching the problem of redressing its trade imbalances with the developing countries, through, for example, "development-imports" (that is, aid for the development of resources that could be imported by Japan). Japan is also considering, together with the other developed countries, granting tariff preferences to the exports of the developing countries.

Throughout Japan's aid program, primary emphasis has been and will continue to be placed on the Asian region. At the same time, Japan will also extend all possible economic cooperation to assist the self-help efforts of the developing countries in other regions of the world.

Promoting International Interchange

If a peaceful and affluent society is to be established throughout the world, Japan realizes that there must be a much greater degree of international interchange of goods

◀ *Kyoto International Conference Hall: main Conference Room (above) and overall setting on the shores of Lake Takara (below).*

and capital, of science and technology and of thought and ideas.

To date, Japan has been actively participating in various international organizations with the object of contributing to the development of a free and stable international economy.

In 1955, Japan joined the General Agreement on Tariffs and Trade (GATT) and was host to the organization's 15th General Assembly in Tokyo in 1959. Later, in 1964, Japan became an Article 8 nation of the International Monetary Fund and a full member of the Organization for Economic Cooperation and Development (OECD). The 1964 annual meetings of the boards of governors of both the IMF and the World Bank were held in Japan. Furthermore, Japan took a positive part in the so-called Kennedy Round negotiations in Geneva from 1964 to 1967 for the mutual lowering of tariff and non-tariff barriers.

Under the growing trend toward trade liberalization in the international market, Japan has adopted a policy of successively easing its import controls, and by April 1970 about 94 per cent of Japan's import trade had been liberalized. At the same time, Japan is continuing its efforts for the early removal of remaining import restrictions and the liberalization of capital transactions in recognition that these moves will not only serve its long-range national interests but will also enable the nation to fulfill its responsibilities as a major industrial nation in the world community.

International cooperation in scientific and technological development is coming to occupy an increasingly important place in the modern world and Japan is devoting its efforts to promoting cooperation in all fields of endeavor, including nuclear power, and space and ocean development, strictly from the standpoint of the peaceful utilization of such resources. Japan is also determined to take an active and creative part in international efforts to relieve and remove the so-called problems of modern society, i. e. such global concerns as environmental disruption and urban congestion.

Cultural interchange is of equal importance in the search of world peace. Japan is already taking part in exchange programs in the fields of culture, fine arts, education, sports, etc., in order to promote mutual understanding among all nations and peoples and intends to broaden its activities in this sphere. As a nation which is preserving a unique cultural heritage from old, Japan has also achieved high standards in the various realms of modern culture and intends to contribute to an even greater international interchange in these fields.

Economic Cooperation

Japan's program of extending economic cooperation to the developing nations of the world has been steadily expanded over the years and sincere efforts are being made to further enlarge and promote its contributions to the economic growth of the developing countries.

The total amount of economic cooperation extended by Japan to developing countries reached $1,263 million in 1969, which means the amount has more than trebled over the past five years. This figure represents 0.76 per cent of the gross national product.

This remarkable increase in the volume of economic cooperation has, of course, been made possible by the rapid growth of the Japanese economy. At the same time, this could not have been realized without the determination and efforts of the Japanese people to extend all possible cooperation to the self-help efforts of the people of the developing countries themselves.

Future prospects for an even greater volume of economic cooperation are bright. The Government, in May 1970, formally decided to make positive efforts to achieve the aid volume target of one per cent of the GNP by 1975, at which time it is estimated that the GNP will be about $400,000 million. While the attainment of this target will require utmost determination, Japan is resolved to promote and implement effective programs for this purpose.

Growth of Japan's Economic Cooperation
with Developing Countries (1964-1969)
(Million U.S. Dollars)

1964	360.7
1965	600.8
1966	669.0
1967	855.3
1968	1,049.3
1969	1,263.1

Japan's Economic Cooperation as a Percentage of GNP (1964-1969)

1964	0.45%
1965	0.68
1966	0.66
1967	0.72
1968	0.74
1969	0.76

In terms of the total volume, Japan ranked fourth among the member nations of the Development Assistance Committee (DAC) of the OECD after the United States, the Federal Republic of Germany and France. With respect to geographical distribution, 67.2 per cent or $848.3 million was extended to the nations of Asia.

Japan's economic cooperation in 1969 consisted of $811.4 million in the form of a flow of public funds and $451.7 million in the form of a flow of private funds.

Of the total economic cooperation by public funds, $435.6 million was in the form of "official development assistance," as defined by DAC, including bilateral grants, technical assistance, direct loans, and contributions to multilateral agencies. The remaining $375.8 million was extended as "other official flows," also as defined by DAC.

Economic cooperation by private funds increased by 21.8 per cent over 1968. It consisted mainly of export credits, which totaled $299.6 million, and direct investments, which reached $144.1 million, exceeding $100 million for the first time.

Along with bilateral assistance, Japan fully cooperates in multilateral forums for development programs in such forms as contributions to the Asian Development Bank, the International Bank for Reconstruction and Development (World Bank) and the International Development Association (IDA).

A significant development in Japan's policy of economic cooperation was the role it played in establishing the Asian Development Bank. Japan formally ratified the agreement establishing the Bank in August 1966 and has so far subscribed $200 million to its funding, a figure equal to 20 per cent

Aspects of Japan's economic cooperation: India Leprosy Center (above left): Manila Electric Company (above right); telecommunications trainees in Tokyo (below). ▶

of the total amount of the capital of the Bank. Japan is one of the two largest subscribers to the Bank, the other major contributor being the United States. In addition to this, Japan has made contributions to the Consolidated Special Funds of the Bank: $20 million to the Agricultural Special Fund in December 1968 and $20 million to the Multi-Purpose Special Fund in November 1969.

Technical assistance is another important element in Japan's economic cooperation program. The purposes of technical assistance are to supply the developing countries with technical and managerial skills in order to develop human resources, to increase productivity, to promote scientific research, to raise technical levels and thus· to contribute to the promotion of economic development and the betterment of the people's well-being in these countries. Thus, Japan is actively providing skills and techniques in agriculture, transportation and communications, light industries, and medical and health care.

In fiscal 1969 (ending March 1970), Japan dispatched 426 experts to the developing countries for a total of 2,237 experts since 1955. Japan also accepts trainees from abroad in many technical and scientific fields. A total of 12,489 trainees had been received as of March 1970, including 1,591 for the 1969 fiscal year.

In addition, Japan donates medical equipment, medicines and other medical supplies to the developing countries to help fight debilitating and often deadly diseases. In fiscal 1969, these donations totaled $782,000, being extended to twenty countries.

Aside from experts, Japan sends many young people under the program of the Japan Overseas Cooperation Volunteers to work in the fields and factories, schools and clinics together with the youths of the developing countries.

One highlight of Japan's technical assistance program is the establishment of technical training centers, staffed by teachers and instructors from Japan. As of the end of 1969, a total of thirty-one centers were in

◀ The Nam Ngum Dam in Laos being built with technical and economic cooperation from Japan and other countries.

operation, providing research and training in such fields as agriculture, fishery, textile industries, small-scale industries and telecommunications.

DEFENSE

The maintenance of Japan's national defense is based upon two elements: the Self-Defense Forces and the collective security system with the United States. The security system was initiated in 1951 with the "Security Treaty between Japan and the United States of America," concluded at the time of the signing of the San Francisco Peace Treaty. The present system exists under the terms of the "Treaty of Mutual Cooperation and Security between Japan and the United States of America," concluded in 1960, which supplants the earlier pact. This Treaty provides, among other details, for the stationing of U.S. military forces within Japan "for the purpose of contributing to the security of Japan and the maintenance of international peace and security in the Far East."

In the initial years of the mutual security system, the U.S. military forces were a major factor in the nation's defense. Today, they have come to play a supplementary role as the Self-Defense Forces have developed a greater defensive capability.

Prior to 1950, Japan was totally without arms and its security, both internal and external, rested wholly with the occupying forces of the Allied Powers, the majority of which were from the United States. The outbreak of hostilities in Korea created a serious security vacuum in Japan when the American forces stationed in Japan were sent to the war theater. On the initiative of the occupying powers, it was decided that the Japanese should assume part of the responsibility for their internal security.

Accordingly, in July 1950, the Supreme Commander for the Allied Powers in Tokyo instructed the Japanese Government to set up a National Police Reserve of 75,000 men and to increase the strength of the Maritime Safety Agency—approximately equivalent to a coastguard force—to 18,000 men. These became the embryo of what are today the Self-Defense Forces.

With the establishment of the mutual

security system with the United States in 1951, Japan's defense capability was steadily enhanced. The Police Reserve and the Maritime Safety Agency were transformed into the Ground Self-Defense Force and the Maritime Self-Defense Force, respectively, while the Air Self-Defense Force and the Japanese Defense Agency have been established. In July 1956, the National Defense Council was organized to act as the highest advisory group available to the Prime Minister on matters relating to the nation's defense policy.

As a result of successive build-up programs, the Self-Defense Forces, as of January 1970, had a total of 258,074 uniformed personnel in its three services. The breakdown was as follows:

Joint Chiefs of Staff: 78 uniformed personnel.

Ground Self-Defense Force: 179,000 uniformed personnel and 33,000 uniformed reserve personnel. The GSDF is organized in five armies, 13 divisions. The GSDF has 350 aircraft and 105 missile launchers.

Maritime Self-Defense Force: 37,813 uniformed personnel with 210 ships and other vessels, aggregating approximately 133,000 tons, 155 anti-submarine aircraft and 100 miscellaneous aircraft.

Air Self-Defense Force: 41,138 uniformed personnel. The ASDF has 970 aircraft, including F-104Js and F-86Fs, and 75 missile (Nike) launchers, which are under the BADGE (base air defense ground environment) system.

Under the third five-year Defense Build-up Program, currently running until fiscal 1971, the Self-Defense Forces have been strengthening their defense capabilities, with main emphasis on a qualitative improvement in weapons and other equipment of the Self-Defense Forces rather than an increase simply in numbers. Among the weapons and equipment introduced under this program, there are, for example, surface-to-air missiles (Nike and HAWK), F-4FJ Phantom and anti-submarine aircrafts.

In both its treaty arrangements with the United States and its own defense preparations, a factor that is constantly borne in mind is the limitations presented by the war-renunciation clause of the Constitution. The Supreme Court ruled in 1959 that the Con-stitution presented no impediment to the exercise of Japan's inherent right to defend itself against aggression. A corollary of this is that both in its treaty and its own defense arrangements, Japan's preparations are limited to purely defensive measures.

The Security Treaty with the United States expressly states that it will be implemented within the constitutional limitations presented by the war-renunciation clause. The Self-Defense Forces are themselves armed only with defensive weapons. The Air Self-Defense Force, for example, has no long-range bombers, and the Maritime Self-Defense Force has no combat ship bigger than a destroyer. It is also basic policy that the Self-Defense Forces shall not be sent overseas.

Elements of the Self-Defense Forces: F-104J fighters of the ASDF (above) and destroyers of the MSDF (below).▶

ECONOMY

BACKGROUND

Japan is a small island country, poorly endowed with natural resources and supporting a massive population of more than 100 million. Yet, despite these limiting conditions, and the devastation of its industrial structure during World War II, Japan has managed not only to rebuild its economy, but to achieve a rate of economic growth that, in the span of a mere quarter of a century, has brought the nation to the third-ranking position in the world in terms of economic scale. This process of rehabilitation and subsequent growth stems from numerous factors that have served to bring the economy up to the present day. This same process has also given rise to various problems that the economy must now face as Japan moves into the decade of the seventies.

Postwar Growth

At the end of World War II, Japan lost all of its overseas territories while its population soared beyond the 80 million mark with the addition of some six million repatriates from abroad. The food supply was at the minimum level, sometimes less.

◀ *Tokyo immediately following the end of the war (above).*
Tokyo today as seen from the Imperial Palace Plaza toward the Marunouchi business district (below).

Production facilities had suffered heavy damage and about one-third of the national wealth accumulated as a result of industrialization since the Meiji Era was lost.

Recovery became the urgent and immediate goal and the people devoted the whole of their energies to this task. Assistance from the United States substantially helped the people start their recovery in the immediate postwar years. Supplies of American food saved the people from starvation, while the American Aid Counterpart Fund became an important source of funds for Japanese enterprises during the rehabilitation period.

This combination of the people's strenuous efforts and American assistance, coupled with a relatively favorable international setting, enabled the Japanese economy to recover with great rapidity. After reaching its prewar level in less than 10 years, the economy continued to grow at an accelerated pace.

The average annual growth rate of Japan's gross national product (GNP) from the start of the Meiji Era to just prior to World War II stood at an estimated 4 to 5 per cent in real terms. Following the war, this rate reached 9.0 per cent in the 1950's and 11.2 per cent in the 1960's. That is, Japan's economy expanded two to three times as fast as other principal industrial nations. The 1969 estimated GNP stood at $166,400 million. Although this ranks second in the free world after the United States, it is still less than one-fifth of the American GNP of $932,100 million for the same year.

Year	GNP (U.S. $ billion)	Per Capita National Income (US $)
1950	10.9	123
1955	24.0	198
1960	43.0	356
1965	88.3	707
1968	141.9	1,122
1969	166.4	1,289

Japan's Gross National Product and Per Capita National Income

The production of mining and manufacturing underwent a spectacular recovery. Having dropped to 27.6 per cent of the prewar level (1934-36) in 1946, it rose steadily, surpassing the prewar level in 1951, and climbed to 3.5 times that level by 1960. Then during the sixties, production climbed nearly fourfold so that today Japan ranks among the leading producers of principal industrial goods: first in the production of ships and radios, second in automobiles, television sets and rubber products, and third in cement and iron and steel.

With the rapid expansion of the domestic economy, Japan's external trade also registered a continued smooth growth against a background of expanding world trade based upon the principle of free trade. Exports have risen at an average annual rate of 16.5 per cent during the past 10 years, a figure almost double the average growth rate of world trade. In 1969, Japan's export trade totaled $16,000 million and the share in aggregate world exports (excluding the Communist countries) soared from 3.6 per cent in 1960 to 6.6 per cent, although this accounts for only 9.6 per cent of Japan's GNP and is about half as much as the ratio for Great Britain or the Federal Republic of Germany.

The nation's imports have followed a similar pattern of steady growth. From a figure of $4,500 million in 1960, imports surged nearly fourfold to reach $15,000 million in 1969, representing 5.9 per cent of total world imports for that year. This increase clearly indicates the tremendous expansion of the domestic market for consumer and industrial products.

Since the latter half of the 1950's, the rapid growth in importance of the heavy and chemical industries in Japan's industrial structure has come to be reflected in the nation's export trade. This shift also gave added impetus to the growth of Japanese exports. Early in the 1950's, light industrial products still accounted for about half of Japan's export value. By 1965, however, the proportion of heavy and chemical industrial products had increased to 61 per cent of total export value and risen to about 69 per cent in 1969.

The change in import trade composition also is indicative of how the economy has changed. The importance of such goods as food and machinery, major imports in the immediate postwar years, has diminished. Instead, raw materials for industrial use now account for as much as 70 per cent of Japan's total imports. At present, Japan is one of the largest importers of raw materials in the world.

The shift in Japan's balance of payments position also reflects the great changes in the economy. For years after the end of the war, the balance of payments was marked by the pattern of a surplus in capital transactions compensating for a deficit in the current account. As the economy steadily strengthened its competitive position in world markets, the trade balance gradually improved. At the same time, with an increase in the outflow of capital due to credits for deferred payments parallel to the growth of Japan's exports as well as the nation's stepped-up foreign aid, the balance of long-term capital transactions deteriorated. As a consequence, with 1965 as the turning point, Japan's balance of payments position assumed the pattern of a surplus in the current account offsetting a deficit in long-term capital transactions.

Japan's foreign exchange reserves reached the $2,000 million level in April 1961, but lingered below that point for a long time. Successive surpluses in the balance of payments in 1968 and 1969, however, increased the holdings to $3,500 million as of the end of 1969.

Factors in Development

Behind the remarkable development of the Japanese economy in postwar years stand various factors. As already noted, the Japanese economy not only recovered its prewar level in less than ten years, but also continued to grow thereafter at an even faster pace. This pace was made possible chiefly by factors stemming from conditions inherent in Japan's socio-economic structure itself. The more important of these are outlined below.

Democratization

A series of measures to democratize the nation's economic and social systems were carried out after the war. For example, the dissolution of the "Zaibatsu" (large financial trusts), the enactment of labor laws for

Mammoth cranes capable of carrying 600-ton loads at a shipyard in Nagasaki.▶

promoting the growth of labor unions and establishing a modern labor-management relationship, and land reform which enabled tenant-farmers to obtain their own land. These brought about a more equal distribution of wealth and income and removed the obstacles to free competition, thereby establishing an economic system which respects the originality and entrepreneurship of the private sector. The foundation was thus laid for the expansion of the domestic market and the rapid development of highly sophisticated industries. At the same time, the people's enterprising spirit was brought into full play as the prime force in economic reconstruction.

Investment and Savings

This spirit found application in the relatively young executives who took over corporate management after the war. They actively and resolutely invested in new equipment to modernize the destroyed or worn-out facilities as well as to survive in a highly competitive domestic market. Banking institutions responded to their needs and provided the necessary funds. At the same time, the people continued to follow the tradition of thrift with the result that the personal savings ratio was as high as 20 per cent. These savings were funneled through the banks to private enterprises, enabling Japanese industries to invest heavily without relying too much upon borrowings from abroad. As a result of this pattern of borrowings for equipment investment, the capital composition of Japanese enterprises is marked by the preponderance of borrowed capital. Owned capital accounts, on the average, for only 20 per cent of total capital today. Increasing the ratio of owned capital has now emerged as a major task for the future.

◄*System engineer using graphic display system with light-pen (above).*
Drafting blueprints for a rotary-engine automobile (below).

Technological Innovation

In an effort to fill the technological gap resulting from the war, industry undertook to introduce foreign technology on a wide scale and then moved ahead to develop a unique technology of its own. This not only brought about a sophistication of Japan's industrial structure through the elevation of labor productivity in those sectors where foreign technology was introduced, but it also stimulated further equipment investment, thus providing a major impetus to the rapid growth of the economy.

In this process, technological interchange between Japan's large enterprises and those of medium and small scale grew rapidly on the domestic scene, while, internationally, Japan has gradually come to export its own technological developments to other nations.

Parallel to such a diversification of technological interchange, efforts have been stepped up in recent years to enlarge production facilities in order to seek the advantages of big scale, against the background of the growing labor shortage and progress in trade and capital liberalization. Technological innovation and investment to save labor and promote automation is making rapid headway. Research and development is gaining momentum and newly-developed techniques in one field are inducing and multiplying technological innovations in others.

Labor Supply

The availability of a large well-educated and well-disciplined labor force contributed immeasurably to the reconstruction of the economy and its subsequent growth. In the course of Japan's rapid economic development after the war, the demand for labor rose sharply, centering on the modern industries. At the same time, the supply of new labor increased with the expansion of the productive-age population and much greater labor mobility. A major contributing factor to the supply of labor in those years was the widespread and heavy outflow of the agricultural population to industry.

Changes in Ratio of Employed Workers (Per cent)			
Year	Primary Industry	Secondary Industry	Tertiary Industry
1955	40.2	24.0	35.9
1960	32.5	27.8	39.8
1965	25.5	31.6	42.8
1969	18.8	34.0	46.1

In recent years, however, a growing shortage of labor has appeared, especially among young workers, as a result of the postwar decline in the birth rate and a rise in the ratio of secondary school graduates advancing to institutions of higher learning. Thus Japan's advantage in labor supply is being gradually lost.

Other Factors

The rather favorable international environment which has surrounded Japan since the end of the war enabled Japan's foreign trade to grow smoothly. In addition, Japan has been able to obtain needed raw materials from various parts of the world, while most of its industrial plants have been built along coastal areas, thereby taking advantage of low costs for imported raw materials from all over the world.

Another factor which also contributed to Japan's postwar economic growth has been the low costs of defense because of the special position in which Japan was placed after the war.

Prospects and Problems

While the rapid growth of the past quarter century has given Japan a gross national product of $166,400 million in 1969, second in the free world, the per capita national income stood at only $1,289 in 1969, placing Japan 15th or 16th in the free world, lower than the levels of the industrialized nations in Europe and North America. Moreover, the rapid growth of the Japanese economy has brought forth various imbalances: for instance, a relative delay in modernizing such areas as agriculture and medium- and small-scale enterprises; the sustained uptrend of consumer prices; the shortage of social overhead capital, such as housing, roads and other facilities of the living environment; increased public hazards; overcongestion of the cities and a depopulation trend in rural areas; and the destruction of nature and increased social tensions arising from progress in mechanization.

The problem facing the Japanese economy is how to resolve these economic and social problems while raising the productivity of the economy as a whole.

Although all countries are seeking further economic growth, the nations of Europe and North America can undertake this task while enjoying an affluent life built upon a national wealth accumulated in the past. Japan has yet to attain that level. Rather, Japan must seek to maintain economic growth at an appropriate pace while ensuring that the fruits of such growth will be equitably distributed among the people in order to build a society satisfying in human terms.

This process must also be accompanied by a greater degree of internationalization of the economy than at present. The internationalization of the Japanese economy started somewhat later than in Europe and North America. However, in view of the large scale of the Japanese economy today and the nation's international stature, strong demands have arisen that Japan should liberalize its external trade and capital transactions and increase its economic cooperation with other nations.

An expanding world economy is an indispensable precondition for the growth and development of the Japanese economy itself. Japan must make positive moves in its external policies, such as trade and capital liberalization and aid to developing nations, while striving to consolidate the domestic structure so as to harmonize it with economic internationalization. This calls for removing the various restraints on growth in such aspects as land utilization, labor mobility, raw material and energy sources, the means of transport, etc. It also calls for expanding and diversifying human abilities so that the nation can better adjust to progress and change in science and technology, centering on independent and original

Japan's first skyscraper: the 36-story Kasumigaseki Building in central Tokyo.▶

development, in order to keep pace with the rapid evolution of the "information age" and even greater technological innovation in the future.

Thus, the major task facing the Japanese economy in the 1970's is to build a society which is harmonious both internally and externally by overcoming the various dissonances that have arisen out of the rapid progress and development of the past decade.

NATURAL RESOURCES

Agriculture

During Japan's postwar period of rapid industrial growth, the nation's agricultural sector has undergone vast and far-reaching changes. The process is continuing, bringing about significant improvements affecting the well-being of the farming community as well as the national economy as a whole. At the same time, however, changes have created new problems and difficulties requiring constant review and attention.

Japan was once well known for the large number of farmers in its total population. In fact, the farm labor force accounted for 50 to 60 per cent of the total working population before World War II. Even after the war, the ratio continued around 40 per cent for some time, but from the latter half of the 1950's, a population exodus from rural to urban areas gathered momentum in response to an increased demand for labor by the rapidly expanding industrial sector.

The total agricultural population diminished from 37 million in 1955 to 27 million in 1968, which represented 27 per cent of the total population. The proportion of the farm labor force in Japan's total working population also decreased from 23 per cent in 1963 to 19.4 per cent in 1966, dipping below the 20 per cent mark for the first time, and stood at 18 per cent, or 9.8 million, in 1968. Moreover, the key agricultural labor force, particularly the number of male farmers, is diminishing and the 20-to-39 year-old group is drastically decreasing.

◀Mechanized harvesting of the rice crop.

Owing to the country's mountainous topography, arable land is extremely limited. Only 15.6 per cent, or about 5.8 million hectares, of the total area represents agricultural land, of which paddy fields occupy 58.8 per cent.

Farming plots are intensively cultivated and every square inch of available land is put under crops. Terrace farming is widely practiced to bring even hills and small mountains under cultivation. This small size of Japanese farms once made it difficult to use tractors and other large farm machines, except in Hokkaido where arable land per farm is more plentiful.

The rapid develoment of mechanized farm implements, however, has helped alleviate this drawback and nearly 93 per cent of all farm households are using power tillers and other machinery in paddy rice growing, while, at the same time, 96 per cent of all paddy rice land is being cultivated with such machines.

The average annual increase rate of rice yield per hectare has been 1.6 per cent for the last 10 years and the average yield per hectare stands at 4.5 tons for the last two years.

In contrast with the rapid reduction of the agricultural population, the number of farm-households decreased only slightly from 5.99 million in 1960 to 5.35 million in 1968, of which only 20 per cent were entirely dependent on agriculture for their livelihood, while 31.1 per cent had members holding part-time jobs in the manufacturing or service industries and 48.8 per cent primarily relied on non-agricultural industries. The ratio of agricultural income to total farm-household income decreased from 55 per cent in 1960 to 46 per cent in 1968.

As a result, the ratio of total farm income to national income fell from 16.6 per cent in 1955 to 6.8 per cent in 1968. But the rise in the income of individual farmers, accompanied by a rapid improvement in living standards, can be described as almost phenomenal in recent years. Annual income per farming household has already surpassed the income level of urban households centering on wage earners. For example, the index of income per farm-household was 277 in 1968 in nominal terms with the base of 1960 as 100.

Partly responsible for this income rise is the special Staple Food Control System by which the Government promises the farmers to buy all the harvested rice, bringing the price level of rice in Japan to nearly twice as high as the international level.

Concerning the farm scale, the average holding of arable land was 1.1 hectare in 1968. Farm-households under 1 hectare decreased in number, but still represented 67 per cent of the total in 1968.

As in many other Asian countries, rice production occupies the greater part of agriculture.

It accounted for 46.5 per cent of all agricultural produce in 1968. Land improvement, advanced techniques, improved strains and the heavy use of chemical fertilizers and various pesticides make Japanese farms among the most productive in the world.

In the past three years, Japan's rice harvests have been so consistently bountiful that a yield of 14 million tons is now regarded as normal. Rice output amounted to a record 14,453,000 tons in 1967 and 14,449,000 tons in 1968.

Meanwhile, the nation's demand for food is becoming more sophisticated and diversified. A major change has been the marked increase in the consumption of livestock products, sugar, vegetables, oils and fats, and fruits with a decline in rice consumption. As a result, rice consumption has not risen beyond 12 million tons. This situation is expected to produce an overstock of rice of about eight million tons as of the end of October 1970.

From this point of view, it may be said that the overproduction of rice has led Japanese agriculture to an important crossroad, forcing it to accelerate a transfer to other farm production through hastening an adjustment in the demand-supply situation of rice as well as encouraging more livestock raising and fruit cultivation.

The lack of good pasture land has kept livestock raising on a comparatively small scale. But the production of livestock occupied 20.1 per cent, or second place, in total agricultual production in 1968. In that year, Japan had 1,489,000 head of dairy cattle, 1,666,000 head of beef cattle, 5,535,000 pigs and about 166 million chickens.

Another change in recent years in the pattern of farming has been a very substantial increase in the cultivation of fruits and vegetables, such as mandarin oranges, lettuce and strawberries. Japan, in fact, produces an extremely wide variety of fruits, some of which are exported in considerable volume.

Japan's trade in agricultural products, especially in imports, reflects the great change in domestic consumption. Although Japan was 83 per cent self-sufficient in its agricultural requirements in 1968, a strong and persistently rising domestic demand has caused a corresponding rise in imports, which increased at an annual rate of 12.2 per cent between 1963 and 1968. In terms of value, imports in 1968 amounted to $2,406 million and accounted for 18.5 per cent of all Japan's imports. Chief imports were feed grains (corn, grain sorghum), wheat, oil seeds (soy bean, rape seed), raw sugar, tropical products (bananas, nuts), mutton and fish.

Exports are relatively insignificant (only 1.5 per cent of all exports in 1968), again a reflection of the continuing high domestic demand.

Forestry

Forests cover about two-thirds of Japan's total land area, aggregating 25 million hectares. Rich natural forests are found from the subtropical to the subarctic zones in the long Japanese archipelago. These forests are the main source from which the country derives its principal building material and much of its pulp for paper production.

In recent years, the rising demand for lumber for construction and as a raw material for pulp and paper manufacturing has consistently exceeded domestic production with the result that substantial imports are now required. Imports have risen steadily from a value of $492.5 million in 1965 to $1,274.9 million in 1969; in terms of the ratio of imports to total consumption, the percentage has risen steadily from 28.6 per cent in 1965 to 46.7 per cent in 1968 and about 50 per cent by mid-1969. As a result, Japan has

Logging operations in a national forest (above).
Pasture lands in Hokkaido (below).▶

become one of the biggest buyers of lumber in the world and lumber imports, including lumber-chips, now rank second after crude oil in the nation's import trade.

Principal import sources in 1969, in terms of value, were the United States, the Philippines, Malaysia, the Soviet Union, Indonesia and Canada, in that order.

Of the total forested land, more than 30 per cent represents afforested and reforested areas. The Forestry Agency of the Ministry of Agriculture and Forestry has set forth long-range plans for the preservation of forestry resources, both in terms of industrial needs and the people's welfare. For example, 12 localities within National Forests have been designated as "Natural Recreational Forests."

The most popular species of tree is *Sugi* or Japanese cedar which grows in almost all parts of the country except Hokkaido. Next comes *Hinoki* or Japanese cypress and *Akamatsu* or Japanese red pine.

Fisheries

The seas surrounding Japan have always been rich in all forms of marine life and the Japanese, since antiquity, have taken a substantial proportion of their food supply from these fertile fields. Thus, Japan today is one of the major fishing nations in the world.

The total Japanese fishing catch in 1968 was 8,670,000 metric tons, representing 13.5 per cent of the total world fishing haul.

The industry can be divided into three broad categories: coastal fishing, offshore fishing and pelagic or deep-sea fishing.

Coastal fishing is conducted either by boats of less than 10 tons, by set nets, or through artificial breeding techniques in shallow waters, popularly known as "fish-farming." Although a large number of persons are engaged in coastal fishing (557,000 persons in 1968, or 93.7 per cent of the entire industry), its production amounted to only 23.6 per cent of total value. As a

◄Facilities of Japan's fishing industry: coastal fishing fleet (above) and an artificial fish breeding center (below). Insert: fry of the trout.

result, coastal fishing productivity is about one-fourth that of the larger fishing enterprises, and more recently, fishing grounds for the coastal fishing interests continue to shrink because of water pollution by waste water from factories along the nation's coastal waters.

Pearls, oysters, etc., have so far been cultured in shallow sea waters. In addition, yellow-tail, prawn and octopus are now being raised by the shallow sea culture method and those thus grown are seen on the market with increasing frequency. The rise in the total value of fishery production, which increased by about 55.4 per cent between 1963 and 1968, is attributed mainly to the rapid development of this shallow sea culture program which has been promoted by the Government.

Offshore fishing is conducted mainly by medium-sized enterprises with boats in the 10 to 100 ton class. The offshore fish catch amounts to about 36 per cent of the nation's entire catch, but, in terms of value, it amounts to only 24.5 per cent of total value.

Pelagic or deep-sea fishing is engaged in by large fishing vessels which operate in waters far from Japan. Their catch amounts to about 32.6 per cent of the total catch. Trawling centering on waters off the African continent is conducted by ships of the 1,000 ton class. Tuna fishing in equatorial and sub-equatorial waters around the world is conducted by ships of the 200-500 ton class.

Salmon and crab fishing in north Pacific waters and whaling in the Antarctic Ocean and the north Pacific are carried out chiefly by large fishing fleets with mother ships which act as large floating fish-processing and canning plants.

As a major fishing nation, Japan is acutely conscious of the need for marine conservation and to this end has implemented various measures to regulate the major fisheries, carry out artificial hatching and stocking of fish or shellfish and maintain as well as increase fishery resources. As for the international environment of the Japanese fishing industry, an increasing number of countries have widened their territorial waters or set up exclusive fishing zones along their shores. Such international restrictions on fishing activities have been tightened year after year. To cope with this international environment, Japan has concluded agreements and treaties with other fishing nations for conserving marine resources and has also participated in joint scientific surveys of international fishing grounds.

Mining

Japan is very poorly endowed with mineral resources and lacks most of the minerals necessary to sustain a modern industrial structure, having to import such basic materials as oil, iron ore, coking coal and nonferrous metal ores such as copper, nickel, bauxite, etc. Japan's main mineral resource is coal with reserves estimated, as of 1956, at 20,245 million tons, a mere 0.4 per cent of total estimated deposits in the world. However, this is mostly low-grade bituminous coal unfit for coking and other specialized purposes. Total demand for coking coal in 1969 was 52,311,000 tons of which 51.0 per cent was imported, principally from the United States and Australia.

Twelve other types of minerals are also mined on a fairly wide scale, but most of them are in quantities barely sufficient to meet minimum domestic demand. These twelve are lead, zinc, arsenic, bismuth, pyrite, sulphur, limestone, gypsum, barite, silica stone, feldspar and dolomite.

Domestic output of petroleum is sufficient for less than one per cent of the nation's demand, or equivalent to about one week's supply in a single year. Domestic oil deposits were estimated at only 800 thousand tons in 1969, accounting for less than 0.01 per cent of total world deposits.

This dependence by Japan on imports for oil has stimulated Japanese interests to seek out and develop overseas sources. In October 1967, the Government established the Japan Petroleum Development Corporation in order to supply risk capital to private enterprises undertaking overseas oil exploration. By 1969, twelve Japanese companies, established for this purpose, were operating in 15 areas of the world either in joint operations with foreign capital, through production sharing agreements or under concessions from the country concerned.

Power Resources

The mountainous topography and abundant rainfall give Japan a large hydroelectric power potential, which has been extensively developed. Huge power dams are found in many parts of the country, and in 1955 about 70 per cent of the country's electric power was derived from hydroelectric generation.

Since that year, increasing emphasis has been given to thermoelectric power development, largely for reasons of cost. In 1960, the ratio was evened, but in 1962 the ratio was reversed in favor of thermoelectric power.

In March 1970, Japan had 2,057 power plants, of which 1,560 were hydroelectric and 499 were thermal, with a combined generating capacity of 53,187,000 KW.

Electric power actually generated during the 1969 fiscal year was 273,341 million KWH, of which 74,677 million KWH was generated by hydroelectric plants.

The generation of electric power through the use of nuclear energy has been under study in Japan for a number of years. The first successful generation of power for commercial purposes took place on November 1, 1965, at the Tokai Mura Plant of the Japan Atomic Power Company. The electricity generated by the improved Calder Hall type reactor stands at 166,000 KW.

The Japan Atomic Power Company completed the construction of its second atomic power station, the Tsuruga Plant, in September 1969. This new facility with a light water reactor reached its maximum output of 322,000 KW in December 1969. Electric power companies are also constructing four additional plants. Total atomic power output in Japan at the end of fiscal 1975 (March 1976) is projected to reach over six million kilowatts.

The continually increasing use of electrical appliances in Japanese homes and the rapid expansion of the country's industries

Mammoth dam under construction for hydroelectric power generation.▶

have led to an almost fivefold increase in demand for electric power over the past 15 years. The average growth rate of this demand, some 12 per cent a year, is rather high by international standards, and now Japan ranks next only to the United States and the Soviet Union in generating capacity and annual power output.

Gas as a power source has been growing in importance over the years. Gas consumption in Japanese cities is increasing at an annual rate of about 10 per cent. The largest consumer is the household, accounting for 62 per cent of total demand, followed by commercial establishments, 20 per cent, industries, 12 per cent, and others, 6 per cent. Japanese gas companies have succeeded in reducing production costs sharply by changing from coal to petroleum as the major raw material source.

At the same time, natural gas is attracting considerable attention as a new raw material in view of its low sulphur content. However, lacking natural gas resources, Japan began importing large quantities in the form of liquefied natural gas in November 1969 from Alaska in the United States. A large storage base and cold-storage carriers to transport the natural gas have already been constructed.

INDUSTRY

Metal Industry

Japan's metal industry, especially its iron and steel production, has expanded remarkably since the war. In 1969, output of crude steel amounted to 82,160,000 tons in comparison to 40 million tons produced five years ago. Japan is now the world's third biggest steel producer, following the United States and the Soviet Union.

Japan's iron and steel industry depends heavily on imports for its key raw materials such as iron ore, coking coal and steel scrap. In 1969, Japan imported about 83 million tons of iron ore, principally from Australia, India, Chile, Peru and Malaysia, 4 million tons of scrap iron, mainly from the United

States, and 39.9 million tons of coking coal, mostly from the United States and Australia. The coke consumption per ton of pig iron, an accepted standard of steelmaking technology, is considerably lower in Japan than in other major steel-producing countries.

The extraordinary growth of Japan's steel industry results from the tremendous progress made in modernizing equipment and plant and in introducing new technology, both imported and domestically developed. A total of nearly $10,000 million had been invested up to the end of 1969 in modern equipment and facilities. The industry today can boast of large blast furnaces, widespread use of LD converters and a high degree of efficiency in the operation of strip mills.

Production figures illustrate the successful development of the industry: hot-rolled stainless steel output rose nine times from 101,000 tons in 1959 to 928,000 tons in 1969; LD steel production totaled 63,191,000 tons, a 28 per cent increase over 1968; ordinary steel products (steel pipes, wide strips and sheets, shapes and bars) increased by 20.5 per cent over 1968 to 67,060,000 tons, while special steel products (plates and hot- and cold-rolled sheets) registered a 27 per cent increase to a total of 6,577,000 tons.

LD steel production accounted for 74 per cent of Japan's entire crude steel output in 1968, the highest percentage in the world. In terms of facilities, Japan has 17 hot strip mills and 58 cold strip mills, second in number only to the United States, and the world's largest blast furnace which can produce 7,000 tons of pig iron a day.

The industry has also developed high strength steel, weather resistant steel and surface-treated steel sheets. Super-size wide flange beams have also been developed and are being widely used in the construction of skyscrapers and high-rise buildings which are appearing in Japanese urban centers in increasing number.

Among the non-ferrous metals, Japan produced 629,155 tons of copper and 564,995 tons of aluminum, 712,187 tons of zinc and 186,615 tons of lead in 1969.

The non-ferrous metal industry is registering steady expansion along with growing demands from such high growth industries as automobiles, electric appliances and build-

◀ *Automated hot rolling steel mill.*

ing construction.

Machinery Industry

Evidence of the growth, diversification and high technical standards of the Japanese machinery industry can be seen in almost every corner of the world. Ships made in Japanese yards today sail the seven seas. Japanese cameras, transistor radios and sewing machines have established a reputation for quality and are in wide demand in world markets. Japanese cars, buses, trucks and lorries and railway rolling stock are helping to meet transportation needs on five continents. Electrical generators made in Japan are supplying light and power for homes and industries in Asia, Africa, Australia, and North and South America. Japanese spinning and weaving machinery is being used in the development of the textile industry in many countries of Asia and other parts of the world.

Even before the war, Japan was not only self-sufficient in shipbuilding, rolling stock and textile machinery, but was exporting these items in considerable volume.

Since the end of the war, the machine industry has set the pace for Japan's remarkable economic growth. Taking the year 1965 as 100, the production index in the electrical machinery industry as a whole stood at 284.8 in 1969, while that of home electrical appliances had risen to 193.2. The production index in the automobile industry rose sharply to 382.1, while that of construction and mining machinery reached 314.9.

Electrical Machinery

Electrical machinery represents the most rapidly growing sector of the machinery industry. Its spectacular growth has been stimulated by increased demand for heavy electrical machinery from the expanded power industry and the vast heavy industry sector as well as by the remarkable rise in demand for household appliances.

Production of power generators expanded from 52,185 units in 1965 to 195,854 units in 1969. Exports of electrical machinery, in-

cluding electronic products, primarily to North America, Asia and Europe, amounted to $2,419 million, or 15.1 per cent of total exports in 1969.

Electronics

One of the major developments in Japan's machinery industry in recent years has been the phenomenal rise in the production of electronic equipment. Total output of the industry in 1969 reached $7,489 million, representing an increase rate of 42.2 per cent over the previous year.

Consumer electronics, including television sets, tape recorders, radio receivers, and stereophonic record players, occupied 46.7 per cent of total production and registered a major expansion of 52.2 per cent over 1968. The leading product in consumer electronics is color TV sets which are in great demand following the rapid expansion of color telecasting. Production rose by 200 per cent over the 1968 level to reach a total of 4,833,000 units. In addition, the industry produced 34,090,000 radio sets, mostly transistorized, and 7,285,000 black and white TV sets, most of them also transistorized.

In the field of industrial electronics, which includes such products as communication equipment, electronic computers, electric measuring instruments and various types of electronic calculators and broadcasting equipment, production rose by 26.7 per cent in 1969. The output of electronic components is taking on greater importance each year with the 1969 rate of increase registering 43.8 per cent, which represented 25.9 per cent of total production by the industry.

Exports of electronic products in 1969 amounted to $1,986 million, accounting for approximately 82.1 per cent of total electrical machinery exports. The largest export item in 1969 was radio receivers, but the rate of increase in the export of color TV sets and desk-type computers was remarkable, registering increases of 34.9 per cent and 145 per cent, respectively, over the previous year.

Bulbous bow of a super-tanker under construction.▶

The industry as a whole is applying itself to the development of new technology and its application to practical use. Typical examples are a TV electron microscope which permits the subject under study to be projected on a screen, or to be recorded on video tape or even telecast; a magnet diode called SMD, which is several thousand times as sensitive as conventional magnetic semiconductor elements and can be applied to a wide number of uses, such as direct current motors and non-contact switches, etc.

Shipbuilding

Since 1956, Japan has been the world's leading shipbuilding nation. It is also the builder of the world's largest ships, products of a highly advanced technology combined with modern facilities and thoroughly efficient techniques.

There are in Japan more than 1,000 shipyards, of which 28 are major ones owned and operated by 14 leading shipbuilders who account for 90 per cent of the nation's ship completions. The Japanese shipbuilding industry has had a distinct advantage over its counterparts in the rest of the world in that it can handle the complete shipbuilding process from beginning to end in what may be described as a pipeline system.

Techniques being used include electronic photomarking of steel plates, block-welding, one-side welding of shipplates and the semi-tandem construction system whereby one and a half ships are constructed simultaneously in a single dock, reducing the equipment required by one-third and substantially reducing building time and costs.

Great advances have been made in developing automated and remote-controlled ship facilities thus reducing manpower needs while increasing efficiency.

In 1960, Japanese yards launched 1,732,000 gross tons of bottoms, accounting for 21.5 per cent of the total world tonnage launched. The figure for 1969 was 9,303,000 gross tons, accounting for 48.2 per cent of the

world total. Of this 1969 figure, 5,626,000 gross tons were for export.

With the recent tendency toward supertankers and mammoth multi-purpose ships, such as ore-oil carriers, ore-bulk-oil carriers and container vessels, Japan has constructed six mammoth oil tankers of 327,000 deadweight tons, all of which went into service from 1968 to 1969.

Motor Vehicles

The Japanese automobile industry is enjoying steady growth in parallel with the rapid progress of the nation's motorization.

In 1969, Japan's automobile industry was the second largest in the world after that of the United States, producing about 4.7 million four-wheeled motor vehicles.

The industry was already well established in the 1930's with production centering on trucks and other heavy vehicles.

Starting in the early 1950's, the industry began to pay increasing attention to the production of passenger cars and steady progress in design, quality and output has been registered over the past two decades. In 1969, Japan ranked third in the world in terms of passenger car production, which accounted for 55.9 per cent of overall motor vehicle production with an output of 2,611,499 units, following the United States and the Federal Republic of Germany.

Japan's motor vehicle exports totaled 858,000 units in 1969. Until recently, trucks constituted the principal motor vehicle export, but the ratio has drastically changed and in 1969, passenger car exports constituted 65 per cent of total automobile exports. Overseas markets have also undergone a marked change from the developing countries in the early 1960's to the industrially advanced nations in the mid-1960's. Another development has been the growing export of knock-down cars for assembly abroad. Such overseas assembly plants have been established in countries in Southeast Asia, in Latin and South America, in Africa and more recently in Oceania, Canada and Europe.

Another major development in recent years has been the steadily rising technical standards of Japanese vehicles. With great

◀ *Final assembly of an electric locomotive (above) and a rotary-engine passenger car (below).*

improvements in road conditions in Japan, manufacturers have turned from almost exclusive emphasis on roadworthiness and durability and are concentrating on speed and acceleration performance, fuel economy, riding comfort and exterior design. An outstanding example of the high level of performance achieved in Japanese automobiles can be cited in the various awards that Japanese cars have received in international racing competitions: the 1967 Grand Prize of Italy by a Honda Formula I racer, Overall Prize of the 1970 Safari Rally in Africa by a Nissan Bluebird, and the Class Prize of the 1970 Acropolis Rally in Greece by a Toyota Corolla.

Japan is also the world leader in both the production and the export of two-wheeled vehicles, particularly motorcycles. Export sales have increased 23 times between 1960 and 1969.

Rolling Stock

Japan's highly developed network of public and private railways has always ensured a steady demand for the products of the rolling stock industry. Production has been at a high level for the past decade because of extensive development programs of the Japanese National Railways (JNR) and private lines. In recent years, production has shifted from steam locomotives, all for export, passenger coaches and motor-driven cars to electric locomotives, diesel engines and electric cars. Present demand is assured under JNR's third long-term expansion program for 1965 to 1971.

Production of rolling stock in the 1966-1968 fiscal years was as follows:

	1966FY	1967FY	1968FY
Steam locomotives	7	—	—
Electric locomotives	102	81	104
Diesel locomotives	190	309	394
Passenger coaches	2,313	1,997	2,482
Freight cars	9,231	14,834	13,934

Technical standards of Japan's rolling stock industry are rated very high throughout the world. The New Tokaido Line of super-express trains, opened in October 1964, embodies the world's finest rolling stock technology. A standard-gauge double track line, it covers the 515-kilometer distance

(320 miles) between Tokyo and Osaka with no surface crossings, being elevated for its entire length. The 16-coach trains can attain a maximum speed of 250 km/h (155.25 mph). For safety in operations, the line uses the ATC (automatic train control) and the CTC (central train control) systems, virtually eliminating the need for handbrakes.

The industry is using such new materials as steel plates of great tensile strength, stainless steel, light metal alloys, plastics of every description and plastic paints.

Japanese rolling stock is exported to many countries of the world in Asia, Africa and Latin America, etc.

Aircraft

Japan's aircraft manufacturing industry dates back to 1911 and enjoyed a reputation as a leader in aircraft manufacturing in pre-war years. The industry today is producing chiefly passenger planes and light aircraft for private and company use.

Two types of planes have already received international recognition: the YS-11, a 60-passenger short-range turboprop transport, and the MU-2, a six-to-nine passenger turbo-prop multi-purpose plane.

The YS-11 and the MU-2 have been granted type certifications by Japan and a number of countries abroad. Each plane incorporates advances in the development of STOL (Short Take-off and Landing) aircraft.

The industry is also producing other types of smaller planes, such as the 4-passenger Fuji FA-200 "Aerosubaru." This plane is designed for short runs, acrobatic flight and ease in operations and maintenance. The light weight also provides the FA-200 with a superior rate of climb and acceleration compared with other aircraft of the same class.

The YS-11, MU-2 and FA-200 are being exported in increasing numbers as their

Products of Japan's aircraft industry: FA-200 sports plane (above left); MU-2 turbo-prop executive plane (above right); YS-11 turbo-prop transport (center); PX-S flying boat (below).▶

performance and safety records become better known abroad. The number of YS-11s and MU-2s exported reached 63 and 120, respectively, during the five years since 1965.

The industry's emphasis on research and development has resulted in a number of new ideas. Japanese aircraft engineers have brought back into active service the long-missing flyingboat with the successful debut of the new PX-S. Equipped with a wave-controlling device to permit open sea landings even in rough weather and an extra engine for greater take-off and landing power, the PX-S is designed for use in search and rescue operations, transport, ocean reconnaissance and oceanographic studies. In the field of helicopters, the industry is developing a rigid rotor type craft for industrial use.

Currently, extensive tests are being carried out on VTOL (Vertical Take-off and Landing) planes and on jet engines. The aim of the latter tests is to develop a short-range jetliner which is expected to be the successor of the YS-11.

Precision Machinery

The high technical standards and the rapid technological advances achieved by Japanese industries today are reflected in the field of precision machinery. Outstanding examples are to be found in the optical goods industry, including cameras, binoculars and electron microscopes, and in the growing production of timepieces, including watches, clocks and precision timers.

The optical goods industry produces still cameras, movie cameras and projectors, telescopes, microscopes, optical measuring instruments and optical surveying instruments. The production of optical instruments in Japan dates back to just after World War I with emphasis on the designing and polishing of lenses and the manufacture of glass.

The Japanese camera industry has been a world leader since 1962 in terms of annual output. Japan annually produces approximately 5 million still cameras and over 1 million movie cameras, mostly 8 mm. Of the total, approximately 68 per cent are exported. Exports have risen steadily from a figure of 2,310,500 units in 1965 to 3,980,000 units in 1969.

The industry has developed many new optical instruments for use in medical research. These include the phase contrast microscope, the ultraviolet and the infrared microscope, the gastro-camera, the fiber-optics gastroscope and the tele-endoscope.

Japanese binoculars and monoculars, noted for their high quality lenses and precision manufacture, have become major export products of the optical goods industry. The export figure in 1969 was 6,676,900 units, against 4,279,000 units in 1965. Most of the exports are refracting prism types of binoculars. Major markets are the United States, the Federal Republic of Germany and Canada.

Timepieces are Japan's latest entry into the field of precision goods. Exports have risen rapidly from 4,354,000 wristwatches and 3,210,000 clocks in 1965 to 11,300,000 wristwatches and 6,800,000 clocks in 1969.

The high quality and precision workmanship of Japanese timepieces were recognized when the International Olympic Committee selected Japanese products as the official timers for the 1964 Olympic Games. A second recognition came when a Japanese miniature crystal chronometer won six of the seven top prizes in the annual chronometer competition at the Neuchatel Astronomical Observatory in Switzerland in 1964. Since then, Japan has been consistently awarded the prizes in this competition almost every year.

Chemical Industry

The chemical industry represents one of the most important fields of industrial activity in Japan today. In the past few years, output of some individual products has been expanding at 20 per cent annually. Japan now ranks among the world's four top producers of basic chemical raw materials, such as sulphuric acid and caustic soda.

◀*Precision testing of cameras during the manufacturing process (above).*
Petrochemical complex on the Pacific coastline (below).

The extremely rapid growth of the industry has been achieved despite a lack of such essential raw materials as petroleum, salt, potassium salt, phosphate ore and oils and fats, which have to be imported.

The structure of the industry has undergone a significant change in the past decade with the development of the petrochemical industry and the shift in production from chemical fertilizers and industrial soda chemicals to synthetic organic chemicals such as plastics.

The petrochemical industry registered a 10-fold increase in its production index during the 1950-1965 period, and production has continued to rise rapidly, from ¥292,473 million worth in 1965 to ¥897,753 million worth in 1969, and petrochemical products accounted for about 32.6 per cent of total chemical production.

Eleven petrochemical complexes are now in operation in Japan, all located along coastlines. These complexes have been developed in close relation with the oil refining industry which has located on coastal regions convenient to both land and sea transportation routes and near to major markets and centers of demand.

Textile Industry

Japan is still one of the leading textile-producing nations of the world, even though it must import all the raw cotton and raw wool required by the industry, the cotton coming mostly from the United States and the wool from Australia.

At the same time, the textile industry is assuming a proportionately declining role in the economy as the emphasis has shifted from a light to a heavy industrial base. Before the war, textiles accounted for more than half of Japan's total exports. By 1969, they had declined to 14.2 per cent.

In the last decade, synthetic textiles have grown in importance to the economy and, next to the United States, Japan leads the world in synthetic fibre output, accounting for 18.4 per cent of total world production in 1969. On the other hand, cotton textiles and silk have suffered a decline in relation to the textile industry as a whole.

In 1969, the total output of synthetic fibres

amounted to 1,321,000 tons while the production of cotton yarn totaled 527,000 tons and cotton fabrics 2,779 million square meters. Other production figures for the year were woolen yarn, 175,000 tons; woolen fabrics, 434 million square meters; and synthetic fabrics, 3,668 million square meters.

FOREIGN TRADE

The free and open trading community of the world has been essential to Japan's great economic progress. Japan is now a major trading nation and a full-fledged partner in a growing world economy. Not only in its needs for raw materials, but also in the demands for industrial and consumer goods, the Japanese economy depends upon the free flow of international trade.

The following tables show the principal commodities which Japan must import and the degree to which it depends on these imports in relation to total consumption:

Self-sufficiency Ratio of Principal Agricultural Products (Per cent)

Product	1966	1967	1968
Rice	101	115	118
Wheat	21	20	20
Barley	65	59	59
Soy beans	9	8	7
Fruits	89	89	88
Meat (except whale)	90	85	83
Milk & dairy products	80	82	88
Sugar	26	27	26

Ratio of Imports to Total Consumption of Principal Industrial Materials (Per cent)

Product	1967	1968	1969
Raw cotton	100.0	100.0	100.0
Raw wool	100.0	100.0	100.0
Iron ore	98.1	98.5	98.9
Bauxite	100.0	100.0	100.0
Copper ore	89.6	89.9	90.3
Coking coal	66.0	71.4	76.2
Crude rubber	100.0	100.0	100.0
Crude oil	99.3	99.4	99.5
Lumber	38.6	46.7	51.0

Raw materials, fuel and foodstuffs constitute Japan's principal imports. Japan relies on overseas sources for practically all its raw

For Japan's foreign trade: air freight shipments by Japan Air Lines (above) and container shipments from Yokohama's Container Terminal (below). ▶

cotton, raw wool, bauxite and rubber and for more than 90 per cent of its iron ore and crude oil.

The total value of exports and imports on a customs clearance basis and their ratios in world exports and imports are as follows:

(Unit: $1 million)

Year	Exports	Japan's ratio in world exports (%)	Imports	Japan's ratio in world imports (%)
1960	4,055	3.6	4,491	3.8
1961	4,236	3.5	5,810	4.7
1962	4,916	3.9	5,637	4.2
1963	5,452	4.0	6,736	4.7
1964	6,673	4.4	7,938	4.9
1965	8,452	5.1	8,169	4.7
1966	9,776	5.4	9,523	4.9
1967	10,442	5.5	11,663	5.8
1968	12,972	6.1	12,987	5.8
1969	15,990	6.6	15,024	5.9

Japan's exports increased by an average of 16.8 per cent annually between 1960 and 1969, or at a rate about twofold that of world exports. The share enjoyed by Japan in world exports also ranked fourth, next to the United States, the Federal Republic of Germany and Great Britain. On the other hand, the rate of increase of imports was slightly lower, averaging 15.8 per cent for the same period, or a rate 1.8-fold that of world imports. In terms of world imports, Japan ranked fifth after the United States, the Federal Republic of Germany, Great Britain and France, in that order.

Exports and imports in 1967-69 were:

Exports by Commodities

(Unit: $1 million)

	1967	1968	1969
Foodstuffs	372	432	572
Marine products	243	281	273
Textiles and textile goods	1,704	1,977	2,271
Raw silk	4	9	3
Cotton yarn	11	12	14
Synthetic fiber fabrics	313	394	512
Cotton fabrics	248	238	221
Silk fabrics	26	25	23
Woolen fabrics	85	104	94
Rayon fabrics	61	57	50
Spun rayon fabrics	71	67	58
Clothing	336	387	451
Pharmaceuticals and chemical products	684	805	1,016
Chemical fertilizer	179	183	152
Plastic materials	174	216	328

Non-metallic	297	329	389
Ceramic ware	96	115	137
Metal and metal products	1,781	2,347	2,935
Iron and steel	1,272	1,712	2,165
Metal products	403	473	585
Machinery	4,395	5,656	7,123
Textile machinery	106	119	148
Sewing machines	97	115	131
Radios	334	421	580
Automobiles	434	713	984
T.V. sets	164	266	354
Ships	982	1,084	1,137
Optical instruments	314	372	439
Tape recorders	195	272	400
Others	1,208	1,425	1,685
Plywood	69	93	93
Toys	101	113	129
Total	10,442	12,972	15,990

Imports by Commodities

(Unit: $1 million)

	1967	1968	1969
Foodstuffs	1,805	1,879	2,141
Wheat	308	289	297
Corn	219	242	248
Sugar	122	147	198
Textile raw materials	898	952	927
Wool	365	363	392
Cotton	443	511	424
Metal ore and scrap	1,600	1,649	1,972
Iron ore	718	834	969
Scrap iron	312	158	209
Non-ferrous metal ore	486	591	729
Other materials	1,995	2,265	2,502
Raw hides	75	74	102
Soy beans	272	274	281
Crude rubber	89	83	127
Lumber	934	1,161	1,275
Beef tallow	35	35	44
Mineral fuels	2,239	2,675	3,044
Coal	401	518	675
Crude oil	1,457	1,685	1,907
Petroleum products	341	415	391
Pharmaceuticals and chemical products	611	690	783
Machinery	1,053	1,327	1,635
Metalworking machinery	58	143	142
Business machinery	160	179	217
Others	1,462	1,551	2,020
Iron and steel	369	246	233
Non-ferrous metals	590	647	917
Total	11,663	12,987	15,024

Japan's changing industrial structure and new trade and other factors overseas have resulted in a distinct shift both in the substance and the distribution of the country's foreign trade.

Before the war, textile raw materials accounted for 32 per cent of total imports, and textiles made up more than half of total exports. In 1969, textile raw materials accounted for only 6.2 per cent of total imports, while textile exports had fallen to 14.2 per cent of the total export trade.

◄ *The Universe Ireland, a 327,000-DWT mammoth tanker, built in Japan.*

Among raw materials and fuels, there has been a sharp rise in the imports of petroleum, iron ore and non-ferrous metals, reflecting the growing importance of Japan's heavy industries.

Meanwhile, exports of metal products, machinery and chemicals which before the war amounted to an average of only 16 per cent of total exports, had risen by 1969 to 69.3 per cent ($11,074 million), or the same level as those of other advanced countries. Particularly striking advances have been made in the latter half of the 1960's in exports of heavy and chemical industrial products, such as iron and steel, ships, automobiles and radio sets.

In terms of distribution, the Asian market before the war provided the biggest outlet for Japanese goods. Mainland China, India and Indonesia alone took 40 per cent of Japan's total exports.

Today, North America and Asia constitute Japan's major markets. In 1969, North America accounted for 36.9 per cent of Japan's exports and 34.4 per cent of its imports. Asia took 33.8 per cent of Japan's total exports and supplied 30.4 per cent of its imports. Japan's exports to Europe accounted for 15.1 per cent of total exports, while Europe supplied 13.8 per cent of Japan's imports.

Japan's biggest single trading partner today is the United States, which in 1969 took 31.0 per cent of Japan's total exports. Japan in turn is the United States' second biggest customer after Canada.

When viewed from the area composition of exports, those to advanced countries accounted for 52 per cent of the total in 1969, those to developing countries 43.0 per cent, and those to the Communist countries 4.8 per cent. (See inside of back cover for graphs and diagrams.)

TRANSPORT

The rapid growth of the Japanese economy has resulted in a remarkable demand for transportation facilities, and Japan's transport industry has made great strides in recent years by introducing faster, safer and more economical transportation means. These efforts have borne fruit in the completion of the world's fastest train service, the launching of the world's largest oil tanker, and the rapid expansion of international air routes by Japan Air Lines.

Land Transport

Railway transport is still playing an important role in Japan's land transport. But it has now entered a new era of modern transportation with the completion of a vast network of expressways, and highway transport is increasing in importance.

The Japanese National Railways (JNR), a public corporation, is the biggest single enterprise in the country. As of March 1969, the JNR was operating 20,827 kilometers (12,934 miles) of railways and accounted for 39.1 per cent of total land passenger transport and 36.5 per cent of total land freight transport in the country.

JNR is a world leader in transportation research and its most significant achievement to date has been the successful inauguration of the world's fastest trains on the New Tokaido Line. Opened on October 1, 1964, this line provides super-express service in 3 hours and 10 minutes between Tokyo and Osaka, a distance of 515 kilometers (320 miles). At present, these trains run at maximum speeds of 210 km/h (130.41 mph).

Construction has already been started on the New Sanyo Line which will extend the New Tokaido Line from Osaka to the city of Hakata in northern Kyushu. The first section, a 170-kilometer stretch west of Osaka, will be completed by 1972 and the speeds of the superexpresses will be increased to their maximum limit of 250 km/h (155.25 mph). The remainder of the new line is scheduled to open for traffic in 1975. At that time, super-express service will cover the distance of about 1,069 kilometers between Tokyo and Hakata in 6 hours and 40 minutes.

In addition to the local lines operated by JNR, regional rail service is provided by 154 private companies, which as of March 1969 maintained a total of 6,593 kilometers

The Port of Yokohama, the nation's largest and busiest international trading harbor.▶

(4,094 miles) of track. These private companies account for about 18.9 per cent of total land passenger transport and 0.6 per cent of total land freight transport.

The railways are supplemented by extensive networks of bus service both in the cities and throughout the countryside.

The volume of passenger and freight transport carried by road traffic accounts for 42.1 per cent and 62.9 per cent, respectively.

The Government has carried out, since 1954, plans for a national network of arterial expressways whereby 32 routes will be built by 1985, totaling approximately 7,600 kilometers. Technical surveys of the entire route have already been completed.

Of this projected network, a 190-kilometer stretch between Nagoya and Kobe (Meishin Expressway) was completed in July 1965, and the Tomei Expressway covering the 346.7 kilometer distance between Tokyo and Nagoya was opened to traffic in May 1969.

These expressways are now playing an important role in the nation's economic development by linking three of the nation's major economic industrial districts. In addition to the already completed Tomei and Meishin Expressways and the Fujiyoshida section of the Chuo (Central) Expressway, presently linking Tokyo with the Mt. Fuji-Hakone region, highway construction is now making rapid headway in several other regions of the country. In addition, urban expressway networks, one in Tokyo and another in the Osaka-Kobe district, are providing for a smooth flow of motor traffic within these metropolitan areas.

Subway lines are in service in four large cities—Tokyo, Osaka, Nagoya and Kobe. In addition, the construction of a subway has been started in Yokohama with completion scheduled for 1971. Meanwhile, Sapporo, Hokkaido, which will host the 1972 Winter Olympics, is also preparing to construct a subway. Tokyo's six lines covered a total distance of 132.1 kilometers (82 miles) as of December 1969 and Tokyo now ranks fifth after New York, London, Chicago and Paris.

◀ *The New Tokaido Line: a super-express train crossing the Fuji River in view of Mt. Fuji (above); construction of the Sanyo extension, west of Osaka (below).*

With numerous extensions under construction and additional lines being planned, the system, when completed by 1975, will cover a grand total of 277.8 kilometers (172.5 miles).

A practical application of a commercial monorail transport system was initiated in October 1954, with the opening of the Tokyo Monorail, covering the 13-kilometer (8 miles) distance between downtown Tokyo and Tokyo International Airport at Haneda in approximately 15 minutes.

A total of 4,066 million tons of goods and 35,930 million passengers were carried by land transport services in 1968.

Maritime Transport

Japan's merchant fleet was the third biggest in the world before the war but was reduced to a fraction of its former size by wartime losses. In 1946, Japan had only 17 ocean-going ships.

Its total tonnage was restored to the pre-war level of nearly 6,500,000 tons by the end of 1959, and Japan today has the world's second biggest merchant fleet, with 23,987,000 gross tons of shipping in mid-1969, including six containerships in active service on the Japan-North Pacific trade route.

Despite this increase in shipping service, Japan's merchant fleet can hardly keep up with the enormous expansion of the nation's foreign trade. As a result, Japanese ships in fiscal year 1968 handled only 37.4 per cent of the year's exports and 47.0 per cent of imports.

Because of the importance of the merchant fleet to the country's economy, the Government has drawn up a revised six-year program for the construction of 2,050,000 gross tons of ocean-going ships between the 1969 and 1974 fiscal years.

In fiscal year 1968, coastal shipping carried 278 million tons of cargo. This represented 42.1 per cent of the year's total domestic cargo transport, exceeding railways and trucks, which account for 21.5 per cent and 36.4 per cent, respectively.

In the same year, Japanese ports handled cargo totaling 1,354 million tons or 1.7 times larger than in 1965. Meanwhile, the Government has carried out, since 1961, a number of five-year plans for port improvement to cope with the growing volume of cargo resulting from the expansion of the economy and to alleviate congestion at ports caused by the shortage of berths.

Air Transport

Japan is today a major crossroad for the world's airlines. Modern jets and other aircraft operated by a score of international airlines companies constantly arrive at and depart from the nation's two largest terminals, Tokyo International Airport and Osaka International Airport.

Japan Air Lines, founded in 1953, is the sole Japanese airline operating international flights. JAL inaugurated its first international air service in February 1954, between Tokyo and San Francisco. Since then, its routes have been continuously expanded until today it serves all continents. In March 1967, JAL opened round-the-world service by way of New York and in October 1969, agreement was reached between Japan and the United States for the inauguration of the Great Circle route service (the shortest route from Tokyo to New York via Anchorage) by JAL. Meanwhile, JAL has inaugurated independent trans-Siberian services, and began operating round-trip flights between Tokyo-Paris via Moscow from March 28, 1970, and between Tokyo-London via Moscow from June 2, 1970, the shortest route between Europe and the Far East. In 1968, Japan's international air carrier handled 4,720 million passenger-kilometers, or 28.0 per cent more than in 1967, and thus ranked 8th among the 116 members of the ICAO.

Owing to the rapid economic growth of the nation, domestic air transport volume between 1960 and 1968 increased at an average annual rate of 27 per cent.

Four domestic airlines, including JAL, provide nationwide service which links the principal cities of Japan and even offer routes to intermediate points throughout the country.

In anticipation of a larger volume of international air traffic with the more frequent use of large type jetliners and supersonic transports, a new Tokyo International Airport is now under construction at Narita, some 60 kilometers (37.3 miles) east of Tokyo in Chiba Prefecture. The new airport's principal runway will be ready to receive the super-jet liners in 1971.

Tourism

Tourism is an important industry in Japan and strenuous efforts are being made to provide the finest facilities in accommodations and travel for the growing number of visitors from abroad, primarily in order to catch up with the steep uptrend in the number of foreign visitors in the years ahead in view of the growing internationalization of business operations and the recent advent of the age of jumbo jet planes.

More than 609,000 foreign tourists visited Japan in 1969 and the tourist trade earned Japan $148 million in foreign exchange, as compared with around 367,000 tourists and $70 million in 1965.

At the same time, more than 712,000 Japanese visited abroad in 1969 and spent $241 million, as compared with around 266,000 tourists and $87 million in 1965, giving rise to a considerable deficit in the nation's tourist trade balance.

The continued upswing in foreign travel by Japanese, either in groups or singly, reflects the higher standards of living of the people as a whole and the rising personal incomes of the individual. Furthermore, with the high-level growth of the national economy, the Government, since 1964, has instituted a series of measures liberalizing financial regulations concerning foreign exchange for travelers, thereby greatly easing procedures for those wishing to travel abroad.

FINANCE

The Japanese Government's fiscal year begins on April 1 and ends on March 31 the following year.

The national budget consists of the General Account and Special Accounts which

Tokyo's urban transportation network includes: the Tokyo-Haneda monorail (above left), expressways (above right) and modern, well-lighted subways (below).▶

are submitted to the Diet together with the budgets of 14 Government-affiliated agencies.

The General Account for the 1970 fiscal year amounted to ¥7,949,764 million or $22,083 million, an increase of ¥1,210,190 million over the previous year. The increase was largely accounted for by higher expenditures for social security and public works.

The policy aims pursued in compiling the budget were to achieve economic growth with stability, to strengthen the country's economic foundations, to raise the people's living standards and to promote public welfare and security.

Details of the General Account in the 1969 and 1970 fiscal years are given in the following tables:

General Account Budgets (initial) for FY 1969, 1970

(Unit: ¥1,000)

Division	FY 1969	FY 1970
Imperial Household	1,761,681	1,831,684
Diet (Parliament)	18,404,976	19,241,590
Judiciary	42,385,868	48,894,810
Board of Audit	1,870,483	2,314,211
Cabinet	2,782,619	3,273,145
Prime Minister's Office	1,033,933,302	1,220,732,496
Ministry of Justice	82,248,806	94,972,785
Ministry of Foreign Affairs	39,362,019	45,106,641
Ministry of Finance	648,616,522	730,125,858
Ministry of Education	742,228,101	845,587,745
Ministry of Health and Welfare	903,931,741	1,103,520,123
Ministry of Agriculture and Forestry	710,245,296	853,020,443
Ministry of International Trade and Industry	91,613,791	97,260,112
Ministry of Transport	161,860,272	183,042,903
Ministry of Posts and Telecommunications	5,534,658	6,310,624
Ministry of Labor	114,328,623	118,115,253
Ministry of Construction	758,087,479	889,126,498
Ministry of Home Affairs	1,380,366,906	1,687,287,195
Total	6,739,574,143	7,949,764,116

The budget for the 1969 fiscal year represented approximately 11.3 per cent of the gross national product. It was about eleven per cent of the U.S. budget and about 68 per cent of the British budget.

Major expenditures in the General Account were for social welfare (14.3 per cent), education and science (11.6 per cent), public works (17.7 per cent), defense (7.2 per cent) and grants for local governments (20.9 per cent).

◀Brilliant displays of neon lights illuminate Tokyo's Ginza district at night.

The most striking change from pre-war budgets was the decrease in defense expenditures, from 40 per cent to less than 10 per cent of the total budget. But with growing recognition of its own responsibilities for strengthening its national defense capability, Japan has been steadily increasing its defense appropriations at an annual average rate of 17.3 per cent over the past five years.

Tax and stamp receipts accounted for 87.3 per cent of the total revenue in FY 1970, and the ratio of bond revenue sharply decreased to 5.4 per cent from 7.2 per cent in the FY 1969 budget, while earnings from government monopoly enterprises such as those from tobacco, salt and camphor accounted for 3.3 per cent.

The Special Accounts cover a number of specific projects including foodstuff control and postal services.

Banking & Securities Market

The Bank of Japan was established in 1882 as the central bank and is the sole issuer of bank notes. It plays the focal part in determining and carrying out monetary policies formulated by the Policy Board which includes representatives of government agencies, banks and industrial circles.

Bank notes, ranging in denomination from ¥100 to ¥10,000 account for 94.4 per cent of the total currency value. State-minted coins, in denominations of from ¥1 to ¥100, are also in circulation. The average value of bank notes in circulation at the end of 1969 was ¥4,811,400 million.

Private banks, which supply more than half of the nation's industrial funds, constitute the heart of Japan's financial institutions. As of the end of 1969, there were 86 private banks with a total of 6,957 branches including 68 overseas branches.

On January 2, 1970, the Bank of Japan was readmitted to full membership in the Bank for International Settlements (BIS) in Basel, Switzerland. However, starting in 1963, Japan's central bank sent representatives as observers to the monthly BIS Conference as well as its General Meetings held annually in Basel.

This is not only an indication of Japan's

strengthened position in the international monetary system, but it means that Japan has to assume a heavier responsibility for international monetary cooperation.

The history of the securities exchange business in Japan is fairly old, dating back to 1878 when the Tokyo Stock Co. was established. Since then, many changes have taken place in its organization and administration.

After the war, the popularization of securities ownership and the need for protecting shareholders called for the re-establishment of organized and responsible securities exchanges. Thus stock exchanges successively came into being in Tokyo, Osaka and Nagoya in 1949.

The Japanese stock-holding population has now reached the level of about 20 million due chiefly to the rising income level of the Japanese people. This means that one out of every five Japanese owns stocks.

On the other hand, Japan's continuing high economic growth and favorable export performance have drawn many foreign investors to the Japanese stock market. The net purchases of Japanese stocks by foreigners through market transactions jumped from $299 million in 1968 to $730 million in 1969.

In view of this, it is anticipated that the Japanese stock market will enter, before long, a real period of dynamism based upon a broader and firmer foundation, taking on a more and more international character.

Two aspects of Japan's financial world: modern lobby of a commercial bank (above) and the trading floor of the Tokyo Stock Exchange (below). ▶

SOCIAL CONDITIONS

POPULATION

Population Growth

The Tokugawa Shogunate instituted census-taking in 1721, conducting nationwide surveys every six years. From these records, it is estimated that Japan's population remained stable at approximately 30 million during the Tokugawa Period.

Following the Meiji Restoration, the population began to increase steadily as the nation's industrialization progressed.

Between 1872 and 1970, the population grew nearly three times, from 34,800,000 to 103,704,000.

Japan thus ranks seventh in the world in terms of population after Mainland China, India, the Soviet Union, the United States, Indonesia and Pakistan, in that order.

At present, Japan takes its census every five years, the last one being taken in October 1970.

Population Density

The density of population in Japan is 280 persons per square kilometer, ranking this country fifth in the world after the Republic of China, the Republic of Korea,

◀A special playground atop one of Tokyo's big department stores.

Belgium and the Netherlands, in that order.

At present, about 70 per cent of the Japanese people live in cities. Of this urban population, 58 per cent is crowded into the "Big Three" metropolitan areas—Tokyo, Osaka and Nagoya. Medium-sized cities in local areas, including Sapporo, Sendai, Hiroshima and Fukuoka, are also attracting people at a rapid rate.

This concentration of population is a continuing phenomenon. A growing number of Japanese are still leaving the towns and villages of the countryside and moving to the big cities to take advantage of greater job opportunities and to enjoy the urban standards of living.

The population figures of the eight biggest cities according to the October 1970 census are as follows:

	1965	1970
Tokyo (Metropolis)	10,869,000	11,399,000
Osaka	3,156,000	2,980,000*
Yokohama	1,789,000	2,238,000
Nagoya	1,935,000	2,036,000
Kyoto	1,365,000	1,419,000
Kobe	1,217,000	1,289,000
Kitakyushu	1,042,000	1,289,000
Sapporo	795,000	1,010,000

*the decrease reflects a move to neighboring residential areas where the population increase has been substantial.

Birth and Death Rates

The average annual rate of increase of Japan's population before the war was 1.4 per cent. It rose to 1.6 per cent in 1950-51, but has since declined, standing at 1.2 per cent in 1968-69.

The population increased by 1,198,000 in 1969, with 1,893,000 births and 695,000 deaths.

The birth rate was 32.4 per thousand in 1930. Just after the war, it registered a sharp rise, reaching a peak of 34.3 births per thousand in 1947, reflecting the so-called "baby boom" of the immediate postwar years. This rate has since fallen drastically, registering a world low of 16.9 per thousand in 1961. It rose slightly to 18.4 in 1969.

The average birth rate was 20.8 and 17.5, respectively, in the 1950's and the 1960's.

On the other hand, Japan's death rate ranged, before the war, between 17 to 18 per thousand. But since the end of the war, infant mortality rates as well as deaths from acute epidemics, tuberculosis and other diseases have sharply declined as a result of marked progress in medical science and greater medical care facilities.

The death rate dropped to 7.0 per thousand in 1963 and even further to 6.8 per thousand in 1969. The average death rate was 8.5 during the 1950's and 7.0 in the 1960's.

Consequently, the average life expectancy of the Japanese people, which in 1935 stood at 47 years for men and 50 years for women, has increased by more than 20 years, reaching 69.2 years for males and 74.7 years for females in 1969.

Population Structure

Japan's population structure, as expressed by the conventional population pyramid, is undergoing a gradual alteration which may indicate that a profound change will arise in the future population pattern.

Once a typical structure before the war (1930) with the childhood population (birth to 14 years of age) forming a broad base, by 1965 the pyramid had become somewhat distorted as a result of the relatively sharp decrease in the childhood population. In terms of age groupings, the childhood population accounted for 25.6 per cent of the total population, while the ratio stood at 68.1 per cent for the adult population (15 to 64 years) and 6.3 per cent for the aged population (65 years and older).

In 1965, the nation's productive age population—the adult population above the childhood level—reached an all-time high of 67 million. This, however, resulted from a temporary factor in that those children born during the postwar "baby boom" had grown to join the productive age population.

Since that time, the drop in the birth rate has brought about a downtrend in the productive age population. If this trend continues, and indications are that it will, the nation will sooner or later face serious problems such as an intensification of the labor shortage of young workers and the necessity to consider even greater measures to care for an aging population.

LABOR RELATIONS

Labor Laws

Japan's labor-management system underwent re-organization after World War II with the enactment of new labor legislation along democratic lines. These labor laws include detailed provisions concerning the securing of modern and democratic labor-management relations as well as employment practices.

For example, the Labor Standards Law stipulates working hours, paid holidays, safety and sanitation, protection of women and young workers and other minimum standards, which, generally speaking, are not inferior to those of other countries of the world.

The Trade Union Law stipulates provisions concerning the worker's right to organize and to bargain collectively, thereby guaranteeing labor unions the right to engage in democratic labor movements and free collective bargaining.

The Labor Relations Adjustment Law, Employment Security Law and other labor laws and regulations constitute the basic framework of Japan's labor relations, which are generally accepted by society.

Labor Force

Japan's labor force in 1969 amounted to 50,980,000 of which only 1.1 per cent was totally unemployed. The principal distribution of the employed in 1969 was as follows (unit: 1,000 persons):

Agriculture and forestry	8,990
Fishery and aquaculture	470
Mining	240
Construction	3,710
Manufacturing	13,450
Wholesale, retail, finance, insurance and real estate	11,330
Transportation, communication and other public utilities	3,380
Services	7,220

Within the last decade, a significant change

Traffic control facilities in Tokyo: helicopter patrols (above) and central traffic control board at Metropolitan Police Headquarters (below).▶

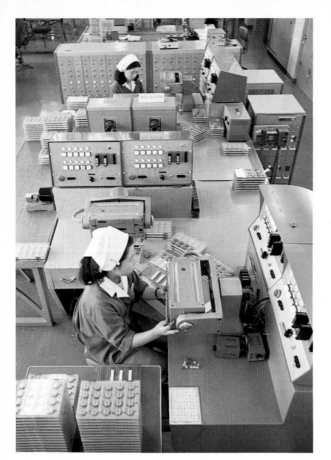

began to appear in the nature of Japan's employment picture with the tightening of the labor market. A labor shortage began to be felt around 1959, despite the massive outflow of the farm population to the industrial sector. While demand for labor has increased conspicuously due to the rapid expansion of the Japanese economy, supply has been limited because of the slow increase in Japan's productive age population and the fact that an increasing number of boys and girls are continuing their studies in high school and beyond rather than finding employment after finishing secondary schools as had been the custom in earlier years.

Wages

Wage levels have been steadily rising by more than 10 per cent for almost every year since 1961, particularly after 1967. This increase has been in parallel with the growth of the economy which averaged 11 per cent per year in real terms over the same period. At the same time, consumer prices have risen at an annual rate of 5.7 per cent for the 1960-1969 period. Price increases have occurred mainly in products of small-scale businesses and the primary industries and in the service sector and in agricultural marketing where increased labor productivity has not kept pace with strong market demand and higher costs, including labor.

Trends of Wage Levels in Japan

Year	All Industries		Manufacturing Industries	
	Index (1965=100)	Ratio of Increase	Index (1965=100)	Ratio of Increase
1960	61.1	7.0%	61.8	8.0%
1961	68.0	11.3	68.9	11.5
1962	75.0	10.3	75.4	9.5
1963	83.0	10.7	83.2	10.3
1964	91.0	10.0	92.0	10.6
1965	100.0	9.5	100.0	8.7
1966	110.8	10.8	111.6	11.6
1967	123.9	11.8	126.3	13.2
1968	140.8	13.6	145.1	14.9
1969	162.8	15.6	168.9	16.4

◀ *Watch manufacturing: precision testing (above left) and parts production (above right). Lessons in the Tea Ceremony for female employees is part of the company's recreational program (below).*

One stimulus behind the rising wage levels is the growing labor shortage, as noted above. Japanese enterprises, in a bid to obtain young workers, have been raising starting wages sharply. This is particularly true with respect to smaller, low-productivity enterprises to the extent that wage differentials, for young workers in particular, have almost disappeared regardless of the size of the enterprise.

Japan's wage-employment practices include a number of rather unique features. One is known as "lifetime employment" whereby young workers who enter a company directly upon graduation normally remain there until retirement. Wage increases are granted regularly according to the length of service. While the labor shortage is tending to weaken this system by increasing labor mobility and by narrowing the wage gap between the new and older employees, this traditional practice is likely to remain for many years to come.

Throughout his working life, an employee is likely to receive semi-annual "bonuses" or "special cash earnings" in addition to contract salary, overtime and allowances. In 1969, the average annual bonus payment for all industries amounted to the equivalent of 3.9 months of regular salary.

Another unique feature is the numerous company-sponsored welfare programs and facilities, the so-called "fringe benefits," which range from retirement allowances and medical insurance to dormitories and housing, child-care, discount stores, as well as medical, educational and recreational facilities. In fiscal year 1968, the ratio of fringe benefits to per worker monthly wage was as high as 18.1 per cent on an all-industry average.

Labor Unions

The Japanese labor movement has made notable advances since the war. In June, 1969, there were 58,812 labor unions with a total of 11,143,382 members.

A feature of Japan's labor movement is that in most cases the unions are organized on a vertical rather than a horizontal basis. In other words, the unions are in general based on a single enterprise, embracing workers of different occupations in that enterprise rather than covering workers of the same occupation in different enterprises on an industry-wide basis. The rate of organized labor for Japan was 35.2 per cent in 1969, the highest figure since 1955.

The majority of Japan's trade unions are affiliated with national federations or associations, of which the two biggest are Sohyo (General Council of Trade Unions of Japan) and Domei (Japanese Confederation of Labor).

The principal members of Sohyo are the public workers' unions, such as the All-Japan Government and Public Workers' Union, the National Railways Workers' Union and the Japan Teachers' Union.

Domei derives its main support from unions in private industry, principally the National Federation of Textile Workers' Unions, the National Federation of Metal Industry Trade Unions, and the Japan Seamen's Union.

The membership of the different national unions groups in June 1969 was:

Sohyo (General Council of Trade Unions of Japan)	4,248,858
Domei (Japanese Confederation of Labor)	1,962,786
Shin Sanbetsu (National Federation of Industrial Organizations)	73,085
Churitsu Roren (Federation of Independent Unions)	1,344,817
Other independent national unions	1,034,410

However, the basic unit of labor union organization and activity is the individual enterprise union. Although efforts have been made to carry out industry-wide collective bargaining with the help of industry-wide labor federations, final decisions are left up to the unions based on the individual enterprise.

Consequently, decisions on wage and labor conditions through collective bargaining cover only the bargaining unions and the management concerned and do not affect others in the same industry.

This form of collective bargaining has fostered a desire among these enterprise unions to deal realistically with the problems of the daily life of the workers and to work in a spirit of co-existence and mutual cooperation with management to ensure the prosperity of the enterprise to which they belong.

FAMILY LIFE

Postwar Changes

Profound changes have occured since the end of the war and are continuing to occur in the family life of the Japanese.

The postwar democratization has infiltrated into every aspect of family life, bringing about various new situations.

A series of measures to democratize the nation's family system were carried out shortly after the war. For example, the Civil Code was revised in 1947 to place women on an equal legal status with men in all phases of life and to abolish the old patriarchal character of the family.

At the same time, the rapid growth of Japan's economy has also had a startling impact on daily living patterns, especially in urban areas. The changes in the cultural and living environment due to advanced urbanization and technological innovation has served to strengthen the tendency toward smaller family units, consisting basically of the immediate parents and children, as opposed to the larger family unit of prewar years.

Further, the widespread practice of family planning in the postwar years has reduced the average number of children per couple to 2.2 in 1967, one of the lowest in the world.

Both husband and wife enjoy equality under law, with equal rights in contracting marriage, in inheriting and owning property, and in suing for divorce.

Mode of Living

The mode of living has also changed under the influence and widespread use of modern household appliances together with the mass production of instant food preparations, a small but steadily expanding supply of frozen foods, readymade clothes and other wearing apparel, and various sorts of daily necessities.

During the 1960's, marked progress was

Family living: a skiing outing in winter (above) and dinner at home (below).▶

registered in equalizing living standards throughout the country and a much greater selectivity developed in the choice of merchandise as well as in movement and leisure for the people.

All this has given additional time for relaxation and educational and cultural pursuits to the entire family, especially the wife who was previously "tied down" to her daily household chores. Thus, under the influence of the lighter household load and increased leisure time, more and more housewives are entering the labor force, although this stems partly from the tight labor market as well.

This rationalization of living patterns and a general leveling of incomes and consumption levels throughout society, plus a change in the people's consciousness through the abundant supply of information by publications and television, has resulted in a growing "middle-class consciousness" among the people as a whole.

A survey conducted by the Prime Minister's Office in 1969 revealed that 81.0 per cent of those interviewed considered themselves in the lower-middle to upper-middle classes.

Consumption patterns indicate this new attitude. As of February 1970, the distribution rate of principal electric and electronic appliances for all Japanese households was 90.2 per cent and 26.3 per cent for monochrome and color television sets, respectively, 91.4 per cent for washing machines, 89.1 per cent for refrigerators, 68.3 per cent for vacuum cleaners, and 30.8 per cent for tape recorders. Slightly more than one out of every five Japanese families now owns a passenger car.

As of June 1969, approximately 94 per cent of all households in Japan had some form of savings and the savings per household averaged ¥1,090,000 ($3,028).

At the same time, the geographic sphere for pleasure and leisure time has expanded and people now travel the entire length of Japan for vacation and leisure activities, while the number of Japanese going abroad for pleasure has been increasing at a rate

Social welfare facilities for the aged: television lounge (above) at an old people's home at Atami (below).

of 62 per cent a year since 1965.

WELFARE

Social Welfare

Social welfare services have been greatly expanded since the end of the war. Especially in recent years, social welfare projects have been high on the Government's list of priorities. In the 1970 budget, the Government allocated ¥1,137,111 million ($31,586 million) for social welfare purposes, or 14.3 per cent of the total budget.

There are also quite a number of voluntary organizations, especially religious bodies, which are providing welfare services to the people in need of help. The majority of such voluntary services are assisted and subsidized by the Government.

Japan's social welfare services cover a wide range of programs including social insurance, public assistance, welfare services for the aged, physically and mentally handicapped, and the care of children lacking a normal home life.

Social Insurance: The social insurance system consists of four programs: health insurance, pension insurance, unemployment insurance and workmen's accident compensation insurance.

Since 1961 the Japanese people have been universally covered under either health insurance programs for employees or those for the self-employed, farmers and the non-employed. Both programs provide medical treatment free of charge, as a general rule, to the insured and half fees for their dependents, in addition to maternity and delivery allowances for insured women. Financial support is derived from contributions by both employers and employees or the self-employed plus subsidies from the national treasury.

Pension insurance is similarly divided into the employed and self-employed and provides cash benefits in the event of old age, permanent disability or the death of the breadwinner.

Unemployment and accident insurance cover all employees except those at small-scale enterprises with less than 5 workers. The former is financed by contributions from both employers and employees, while the latter's expenses are borne wholly by employers.

Public Assistance: The Daily Life Protection Law (1950) guarantees minimum standards of living to all who are in destitute circumstances despite their means of livelihood. The scale of assistance has been raised annually to keep up with the increase in the average level of living among the general public as well as to compensate for the increase in the cost of living. At the beginning of 1969, 1.4 per cent of the total population was receiving assistance under this program. The national government provides 80 per cent of the cost of assistance with the remaining 20 per cent coming from local governments.

Welfare Services: Services provided cover the elderly, the physically handicapped and the mentally retarded.

The Old People's Welfare Law, enacted in 1963, stipulates a number of services including medical examinations, home help services, recreational centers, social clubs, institutional care, etc. In 1968, the elderly population of Japan, those over 65 years of age, constituted 7 per cent of the total population.

Under the Law for the Welfare of the Physically Handicapped (1949), local governments have the duty to provide welfare services for the physically handicapped. These include advice on occupational, social and personal problems arising from the disability, home help service, provision of artificial limbs, wheelchairs, etc., and institutional care for rehabilitation or protection.

The mentally retarded receive numerous services under the 1960 Law for the Welfare of Mentally Retarded Persons, including advice and guidance, training in daytime centers, care in residential homes for the severely retarded, etc.

Children's Welfare: Special arrangements are provided under the Children's Welfare Law (1947) for expectant mothers and young children to receive medical assistance, free of charge, if they are from low income families. Furthermore, there are at present 12 thousand day nurseries throughout the country provided by local governments or voluntary associations, although more are needed to cope with the growing tendency of young mothers to take daytime jobs. For children deprived of a normal home life for one reason or other, care is provided at infant homes, children's homes, etc.

Medical Welfare

The average life span of the Japanese people has risen to 69 for men and 74 for women, levels equal to those of the advanced nations of the West.

While this increase in the life span is due, at least in part, to the improvement in living standards, it is mainly attributed to progress in medical science. Nowadays, modern medical science has conquered the diseases which once threatened the lives of people.

Tuberculosis, which was once considered fatal, rarely is a cause of death today. Also such acute communicable diseases as typhus, diphtheria and scarlet fever have vanished. Also rare are cases of typhoid fever and dysentery.

The Government stresses the importance of preventive medicine and has already established 832 health centers throughout the country as a means of improving environmental sanitation and preventing the spread of communicable diseases in their early stages.

On the other hand, the Japanese people are now menaced by diseases such as apoplexy, high blood pressure, heart ailments, mental disorders, etc., resulting from fatigue and physical and mental tensions, as well as by cancer which today ranks second as a major cause of death after apoplexy.

These "diseases of civilization" are now the principal killers in place of the communicable diseases of the past. Today, Japanese medical science is directing its facilities and talents in the fight to conquer these diseases.

The number of persons per doctor is 898 in Japan, which compares favorably with the ratios in Sweden and France.

Welfare facilities for fatherless families: dormitory living quarters for children and working mothers (above) and kindergarten classes in the daytime (below).▶

However, this ratio varies by locality, being high in urban districts, while insufficient in the remote inland areas or distant islands.

During the postwar years, medical facilities including university hospitals with the most advanced facilities have been rapidly improved throughout the country. With the technological advance of recent decades, medical science has also broadened its horizons and joined forces with various other branches of the sciences, for example, in applying electronics to medicine.

In 1968, the number of hospital beds available for patients was over 1,003,000, that is, about 1.6 times the 1958 figure. Today, the number of beds per 1,000 persons is 10 in Japan.

The following statistics give a picture of Japan's health services at the end of 1968.

Number of Hospitals (1968)

Hospitals	
General	6,579
Communicable Disease	37
Leprosy	14
Tuberculosis	220
Mental	853
Total	7,703
General Clinics	67,962
Dental Clinics	29,489

Health Personnel (1968)

Practicing Physicians	113,630
Dentists	36,943
Pharmacists	74,336
Public Health Nurses	13,560
Midwives	29,440
Clinical Nurses	261,275

Nutrition

Since the end of the war, a major change has been brought about in Japanese dietary habits throughout the country, approaching the pattern of the Western nations.

For example, many Japanese take, in general, their breakfast with toast and coffee. At the same time, the level of nutrition has been remarkably improved, following the elevation of living standards.

The excessive consumption of cereals has diminished with an increasing consumption of meat, milk and dairy products. While expenditures of urban households on foodstuffs increased in absolute terms, Engel's coefficient declined from 38.8 in 1955 to 32.8 in 1969 due to the relatively greater increase in total expenditures than in expenditures on foodstuffs.

The average Japanese consumes 2,454 calories per day and his intake of protein has now reached 75.6 grams per day. Of the total protein intake, 22.4 per cent comes from rice, 38.6 per cent from other cereals and vegetables, 21.6 per cent from fish and 17.5 per cent from livestock products.

LIVING ENVIRONMENT

Housing

Despite the great advances made in creating a more diversified and comfortable way of life, the people are still faced with an absolute shortage of housing. According to a survey conducted in August 1969 by the Ministry of Construction, about 37 per cent of the nation's 26 million households were dissatisfied with their housing situation in one way or another.

Wartime destruction and the rapid increase in the population after the war caused a serious housing shortage. Constant efforts have been made to relieve this shortage and to improve housing standards.

The Government began to subsidize local public bodies immediately after the war in order to encourage the construction of rental housing for low income classes all over the country.

In 1950, the Housing Loan Corporation was established in order to advance long-term loans at low interest rates to individuals who wished to build their own houses. Further, the Japan Housing Corporation was established in 1955, when it became apparent that local public housing programs were unable to meet the concentrated demand for housing in metropolitan regions. The Corporation's main objective is to construct multi-storied concrete apartment buildings on a large-scale in and around the bigger cities where the housing shortage is so extreme.

As for the long-term target, the Govern-

◀Feeding time at an infant's ward (above) and a new hospital exclusively for children (below).

ment established in 1966 the first five-year housing construction plan. The target of this plan is to construct 2.7 million dwelling units with governmental funds or with governmental financial aid from 1966 to 1970.

Since the latter half of the 1950's, the number of housing units built has been increasing at an annual rate of more than 10 per cent, totaling about 13 million units during the past 20 years.

The annual ratio of housing investments to the gross national product also stood high in Japan at around 7 per cent during the past 10 years.

In spite of this, the demand for housing has skyrocketed in recent years as a result of the concentration of population in urban areas and the breakup of families into smaller units, as well as the uptrend of land prices in urban centers which rose sharply by about 3.4 times from 1960 to 1968. In the big cities, therefore, the housing supply still cannot catch up with the demand.

This demand for housing and the rising price levels for land have caused residential areas to spread gradually into suburban and neighboring areas.

In the case of Tokyo, for instance, suburban areas where houses for sale and public housing projects are being built are already located beyond a radius of 30 kilometers from the heart of the city, with some now reaching 50 kilometers.

This has given rise to various problems, such as longer commuting time and increasing difficulties in transporting a greater number of commuters.

Furthermore, since houses for sale are being built in scattered suburban districts, the construction of public facilities, such as roads, service water, sewerage, gas supply, parks and schools, is falling behind.

Prospects & Projects

To cope with these problems, the Government set forth a long-range prospect for housing with 1985 as the target year in the "New Comprehensive National Development Program" announced in May 1969.

According to the Government forecast, the overall demand for housing in the next 20

years is estimated at about thirty million units (including 16,500,000 new houses and 13 million replacements). To meet the demand, ambitious urban rebuilding plans must be carried out on the principle of bringing houses nearer to places of work.

Moreover, the program calls for vigorous urban redevelopment projects for the dispersal and relocation of factories and schools from urban centers to other areas and the construction of multi-story residential structures on the vacated sites. At the same time, the construction of residential areas for large-scale housing complexes, such as "New Towns," must be coordinated with the improvement of commuter transport systems.

Regarding the improvement of the living environment, the national development program proposes a new "public housing formula." That is, although there will be a shift from individual wooden houses to medium and super-high apartment buildings in the heart of big cities, the expansion of parks and the construction of multi-story residential buildings will be undertaken simultaneously in those sectors where areas of "green land" must be preserved.

At the same time, adequate garbage and sewerage facilities will be constructed to create a comfortable living environment. The intention is to improve the housing situation from year to year in line with the policy of expanding social overhead capital.

New apartment houses in the suburbs of Tokyo. ▶

CULTURAL LIFE

EDUCATION

During the long feudal period preceding the Meiji Restoration in 1868, various educational establishments developed to serve the needs of the different social classes. Provincial lords had set up special schools for the children of the warrior class, while rural communities operated certain schools for the wealthier members of the merchant and farming classes. Another type of private school was the "terakoya," where reading, writing and arithmetic were taught to the children of the common people, mostly in urban areas.

Ever since the Meiji Restoration, particular importance has been laid on education. A modern national education system was introduced in 1872, when the Government set up elementary and secondary schools throughout the country. In 1886, every child was required to attend elementary school for either three or four years. In 1900, compulsory education was made free of charge and in 1908, its duration extended to six years. Following World War II, this period was extended to the present nine years, covering elementary and lower secondary schools.

The basic structure and principles of the present educational system are laid out in

two laws passed in 1947: the Fundamental Law of Education and the School Education Law.

A central concept in Japanese education today is to produce self-reliant citizens of a peaceful and democratic state and community with respect for human rights and a love for truth and peace.

Another basic principle enunciated in the Fundamental Law is equality in educational opportunity for all in keeping with their abilities. The Law prohibits discrimination based on race, creed, sex, social status, economic position or family background.

The Law emphasizes the importance of political knowledge and of religious tolerance in the development of sound citizens but it specifically prohibits any link between political parties or religions and education.

Emphasis is laid in the public school curricula on social studies. This is in line with the Fundamental Law of Education, which encourages social education and calls on state and local authorities to establish such institutions as libraries, museums and civic halls.

The educational system is divided into five stages: kindergarten (one to three years), elementary school (six years), lower secondary school (three years), upper secondary school (three years) and university (normally four years). In addition, junior colleges, with courses of two years, are recognized, and many universities provide postgraduate courses for advanced studies.

Education is compulsory for nine years and is provided free for all children between the ages of six and fifteen at all public elementary and lower secondary schools.

As of 1968, 99.9 per cent of the children between these ages were enrolled in schools.

In addition to the public educational facilities available, private schools are found at all stages of the system. These are playing a particularly important role in infant education through kindergartens and on advanced levels, both of which are beyond the scope of the compulsory system. In 1969, as many as 75.6 per cent and 76.6 per cent, respectively, of all pupils and students in kindergartens and schools of higher learning were enrolled in private institutions, while 30 per cent of all upper secondary school students were attending private schools.

The administration of education is decentralized. The role of the Ministry of Education is broadly that of a co-ordinator. Responsibility for school budgets, educational programs, school appointments and the supervision of elementary and lower secondary schools lies in the hands of local boards of education. The members of the boards of education are selected by the administrative head of the local governing authority.

As regards the content of education, each school organizes its own curricula in accordance with the Course of Study, prepared and published by the Ministry of Education. Textbooks are selected by the local boards of education from among those authorized by the Ministry.

School Statistics

On May 1, 1969, the number of educational institutions, teachers, students and pupils was as follows:

	Institutions	Full-time Teachers	Enrollment
Kindergartens	10,418	62,439	1,551,017
Elementary Schools	25,014	361,148	9,403,221
Lower Secondary Schools	11,278	227,405	4,865,206
Upper Secondary Schools	4,817	200,806	4,337,905
Special Schools for Handicapped Children	407	11,429	50,183
Technical Colleges	60	3,081	41,637
Junior Colleges	473	15,445	263,362
Universities	379	74,706	1,354,827

Libraries, museums and other institutions also play a considerable educational role. In 1968, there were 825 public libraries with 23,925,142 books. The libraries were visited in the preceding twelve months by 23 million people. There were also 262 museums, 27 zoos, 31 aquariums and 18 botanical gardens.

In 1968, a total of 9,810 foreign students were enrolled in Japanese universities. They included 4,573 Koreans, 3,087 Chinese and 573 Americans. A steadily increasing number of young people from Asian countries are coming to Japan for technical training at scientific and technological institutes or at various industrial plants and factories.

SCIENCE

Scientific research has made substantial progress over the past two decades in Japan.

At all levels of the educational system, scientific and technical education is an important part of the school curriculum. Approximately 40 per cent of all university students specialize in some branch of the sciences.

In the field of pure scientific research, Japan's two outstanding leaders are Dr. Hideki Yukawa, recipient of a Nobel Prize in 1949 for his work on the mathematical prediction of the meson, and Dr. Sin-itiro Tomonaga, awarded a Nobel Prize in 1965 for his achievements in establishing the "renormalization" theory and its theoretical application to the field of quantum electrodynamics.

Nuclear Energy

The Japan Atomic Energy Commission was formed in 1956 to deliberate basic policy toward the research, development and use of nuclear energy. With the wartime experience of Hiroshima and Nagasaki indelibly imprinted on the minds of the people, Japan's nuclear energy program is strictly devoted to the peaceful application of this new energy source.

Now, with the passage of nearly a decade and a half of research, Japan has entered the era of full-scale utilization of nuclear energy, that is, the peaceful use of nuclear energy is shifting from the research and development stage to that of being established as an industry.

Japan's nuclear energy development center is located at Tokai Mura, 113 kilometers (70 miles) northeast of Tokyo on the Pacific coastline.

Here are located two major facilities: the Japan Atomic Energy Research Institute

Peaceful uses of atomic energy in Japan include: the Tsuruga Atomic Power Plant (above) and the nuclear-powered ship, "Mutsu," shown at its launching in June 1969 (below). ▶

(JAERI) which is responsible not only for research into practical uses of atomic energy but also for the training of engineers for industry, and the Power Reactor & Nuclear Fuel Development Corporation which is engaged in the development of nuclear materials and the research of advanced thermal reactors and fast breeder reactors in order to produce more efficient and economical power reactors.

The JAERI has six research reactors including a material test reactor and a power demonstration reactor. Four universities and two companies are also equipped with atomic reactors for training and research purposes.

Japan's atomic scientists are pursuing the practical application of atomic energy in various fields. Construction of Japan's first nuclear ship was started in November 1967 by the Japan Nuclear Ship Development Agency. The "Mutsu," as the ship is named, has a gross tonnage of 8,000 tons and was launched in June 1969. When outfitting is completed around the beginning of 1972, it will be used for hauling special cargo as well as for the training of crewmen.

In 1969, the number of the facilities which used radioisotopes totaled more than 1,600. The Institute of Radiation Breeding is experimenting with the application of radiation for crop improvement and plant breeding, the Takasaki Research Establishment of JAERI is studying the use of radiation chemistry in industry, and the National Institute of Radiological Sciences is concerned with the medical uses of radiation. In this latter field, many noteworthy techniques in therapy and diagnosis of malignant cancers and other disorders are being developed through the use of various newly produced short-lived nuclides.

In international programs of atomic research, Japan is cooperating in training programs, dispatching engineers and exchanging information and data. Japan is a member of the International Atomic Energy Agency and an associated state of the European Nuclear Energy Agency. Through these organizations, Japan has played its role pos-

itively in exchanging scientific and technical information and specialists. In bilateral relations, there are the Japan-U.S., Japan-U.K., and Japan-Canada Atomic Energy Cooperation Agreements, not only for collaboration on the research and development of atomic energy but for commercial transactions as well.

Space Research

Space research in Japan, which began in 1955, can be classified into two categories: scientific exploration of outer space and the practical application of artificial satellites to such fields as communications, meteorological measurements, navigation, and geodetic surveys.

Developments have moved along steadily and swiftly from the early "pencil" and "baby" rockets to the production of the Kappa series of sounding rockets and the larger Lambda and Mu rockets for space observation. Japan launched 13 Kappa-6 rockets as part of its activities in the International Geophysical Year (IGY) from 1957 to 1958. Thirty-four sounding rockets, including three-stage Lambda rockets, participated in space observations for the International Quiet Sun Year (IQSY) from 1964 to 1965.

For its contribution to the International Active Sun Year (IASY), from 1968 to 1971, Japan is conducting space research with Kappa and Lambda rockets.

Japan's space development projects came into full swing in 1966, when the Lambda 3H No.2 soared to an altitude of 1,800 kilometers (1,118.7 miles).

In 1969, a Mu 3D rocket, an enlarged model of the Lambda rocket, was launched successfully, brightening the prospects for orbiting a satellite.

On February 11, 1970, Japan's first man-made satellite was sent into orbit around the earth. This made Japan the fourth space power in the world to orbit an artificial satellite on its own, after the Soviet Union (1957), the United States (1958) and France (1965). Tokyo University's Institute of Space and Aeronautical Science launched the four-stage Lambda 4S-5 rocket from its Uchinoura Space Center in Kagoshima Prefecture.

◄ *A four-stage Lambda rocket (above) which carried Japan's first artificial satellite into successful orbit in February 1970 (below).*

The Lambda 4S-5 rocket measured 16.52 meters in overall length and 73.5 centimeters in maximum diameter, and weighed 9.399 tons. All of its four stages were powered by solid fuel. The globe-circling satellite consists of the burned-out fourth-stage spherical rocket (48 centimeters in diameter and 13.7 kilograms in weight) with a cone-shaped payload section (9.4 kilograms), containing instruments, attached atop it. The satellite thus measures about one meter in overall length and 23.1 kilograms in total weight.

This satellite, named "Osumi," was registered as 1970-11A with the Committee on Space Research (COSPAR). On February 20, it was also officially listed by the United Nations.

Japan's method of launching the satellite, unlike the guidance system employed by the U.S. and the Soviet Union, was the relatively inexpensive and unprecedented attitude control device which places the last stage on a course parallel to the earth before starting orbital flight. Because of its advantages, it has attracted attention abroad as a unique method.

Equal progress has been made in developing instrumentation for space observations. The "Resonance Probe" has proved highly successful in the direct observance of the ionosphere and has been used three times in joint Japan-U.S. data comparison projects.

Japan's rocket launching site is the Kagoshima Space Center, a 510,000 square meter area on the southern tip of Kyushu. Here are located the Kappa, Lambda and Mu launching pads as well as control, telemetry, radar and optical tracking centers.

Tokyo University's Institute of Space and Aeronautical Science intends to orbit a full-scale scientific satellite in 1970 with a Mu rocket developed for full-scale satellite launching. Meanwhile, the National Space Development Agency, set up in 1969, is pushing forward with a project to send up an experimental stationary satellite in 1974.

Antarctic Observation

Japan has been participating in Antarctic observations since 1956 when an observation team landed on Ongul Island and established its Showa Base. Eleven teams have been dispatched since that date, the latest having departed from Tokyo in November 1969 aboard the specially-designed observation ship "Fuji."

The Fuji is a 7,760-ton icebreaker, transport and floating research laboratory. In addition to transporting 400 tons of food, fuel and instruments for use at the Showa Base, the ship is equipped to conduct 7 types of scientific observations in such fields as meteorology, cosmic rays and geomagnetism.

Japan's Antarctic observation program is concentrating on two main subjects: biology and upper atmospheric physics. Meteorological observations are recorded automatically and continuously through the use of an electronic computer. Special sondes are being used to probe the circulation of air currents above the antarctic wastes. A large-sized snowcar has been developed for observational trips into the hinterlands in the spring months. From 1968 through 1969, the ninth Japanese Antarctic Research Expedition party made history in a research trip from the Showa Base to the South Pole and back with their snow vehicles.

Two test rockets for upper atmospheric observations were launched successfully in February 1970.

INFORMATION MEDIA

Japan has been described as a nation of readers. Newspapers and magazines have large circulations and serve as a vital channel for the dissemination of information throughout the country. An equally vital role is played by radio and television, which are as highly developed in Japan as anywhere in the world.

As of October 1969, there were 116 daily newspapers in Japan. The major newspapers print both morning and evening editions. If these editions are counted sepa-

Editions of Japan's five national dailies and four English language papers (above).
Experimental "TV Home-fax" for transmitting newspapers by radio-wave (below).▶

rately, the total daily circulation is about 51 million newspapers. This means that every household reads, on the average, two newspapers a day. According to United Nations figures in 1968, the total circulation of daily newspapers in the U.S.S.R. was 70 million, in the United States 62 million, in Great Britain 27 million, in the Federal Republic of Germany 20 million and in France 12 million.

A unique characteristic of Japan's newspaper world is the existence of so-called "national papers" with circulations extending all over the country. These account for about half of the total daily circulation. In addition, these national papers incorporate the features of both "quality papers" appealing to limited circles and the "tabloid" type with its mass-circulation approach. Japan's five national dailies and their daily circulations are as follows (as of November 1969):

Asahi:	9,520,000
Yomiuri:	8,770,000
Mainichi:	7,480,000
Sankei:	3,000,000
Nikkei:	1,960,000

In addition to their morning and evening editions, most of these papers publish weekly, monthly, pictorial or other types of magazines.

Aside from these national papers, there are many regional papers as well as sports papers which enjoy fairly large local circulations.

Japan also has regular English-language newspapers available in most major cities: The Japan Times, Asahi Evening News, Mainichi Daily News and The Daily Yomiuri.

A total of 111 newspapers, eight news agencies and 44 radio and television companies were members of the Japan Newspaper Publishers and Editors Association (Nihon Shimbun Kyokai) in December 1969.

The Japanese newspapers enjoy complete freedom of the press. None of the national dailies is associated with any political party or group. Virtually all the Japanese newspapers pursue a politically independent course.

There are two major general news agencies, Kyodo News Service and Jiji Press. Both maintain extensive newsgathering facilities around the world, Kyodo having correspondents and stringers in 30 world news centers plus contracts with 24 foreign news agencies, while Jiji maintains news bureaus in 31 principal cities abroad and has signed contracts with 11 agencies.

Nearly 170 foreign news organizations, including television and radio networks, have resident correspondents in Tokyo.

Besides the newspaper companies, there are nearly 2,600 publishers in Japan. In 1969, they published 26,424 titles and 2,485 different magazines.

Radio and Television

Radio and television in Japan today are as important as newspapers in their function as communications media. At the end of 1969, there were 21,911,000 registered black-and-white television sets and 3,504,000 color television sets in Japanese homes.

Radio broadcasting began in Japan in 1925, when the Nippon Hoso Kyokai (NHK, or Japan Broadcasting Corporation) was established. NHK is a public corporation, directed by a Board of Governors and financed by license fees established by law and paid by television set owners. Radio license fees, once required, have been withdrawn.

As of April 1, 1970, NHK was operating 311 AM radio stations on two networks and 249 FM radio stations which also offered stereophonic broadcasts in many areas. The Corporation also initiated television broadcasts for the first time in Japan in 1953 and today has 987 television stations. In overseas activities, NHK maintains "Radio Japan" which is today beamed in 18 transmissions throughout the world in 23 languages for a total of 37 broadcasting hours a day. "Radio Japan" celebrates its 35th anniversary in 1970.

Commercial broadcasting began in 1951. In April 1970, there were 13 commercial radio companies, 43 television companies and 35 combined radio and television companies. They operate 887 television stations and 155 radio stations serving almost every

◀ *Japan Broadcasting Corporation (NHK): Yoyogi Broadcasting Center in Tokyo (above left); studio production for color TV (above right); and the main TV control room (below).*

part of the country. In 1969, the gross advertising revenues of the commercial broadcasting companies amounted to ¥233,300 million ($648 million). Revenue from commercial television advertising represented 32.3 per cent of Japan's total advertising expenditure in 1969.

Progress in TV technology has been rapid and new advances are being made in cooperation with the electronics industry.

In January 1970, NHK initiated experimental multiple television broadcasts which add another TV voice to the present one. This permits the simultaneous transmission of the TV image and two languages, one the original and the other the translation, or the stereo broadcast of TV music programs. Adaptors for receiving such broadcasts, as well as new TV receivers incorporating the necessary device, are already on the market.

In another radio-TV related development, newspaper companies and electric appliance manufacturers are experimenting with so-called "radio-wave newspapers" by which news can be transmitted directly to subscriber homes where a facsimile-receiving device automatically prints the news or other information sent. Two systems are currently being studied: one using an exclusively-assigned radio-wave and the other utilizing radio-waves currently carrying television and FM radio broadcasts.

LITERATURE

Contemporary Japanese literature, like much else in Japan, draws its strength from a rich variety of sources, from the classic influences of ancient China, from the diversity of Western thought and from the enduring qualities of its own traditions.

A profound influence is exerted to this day by the two oldest surviving literary works in Japan. One of these is the *Kojiki* (Ancient Chronicle), a prose work believed to have been written in 712 A.D. The other is the *Mannyoshu*, an anthology of poems compiled in 770 A.D.

The ninth century was a period of direct contact between Japan and China, and Chinese classics were the moulding influence on the literature of the time. Contact was subsequently broken off and a period followed in which the influence of foreign works was assimilated and Japanese writers evolved a literature of their own.

Taketori Monogatari, which was written around 811 A.D., is regarded as Japan's first novel. It was followed by *Genji Monogatari* (The Tale of Genji), which is a love story and depicts 11th century court life. It was written by one of the court ladies, most of whom were writers and poetesses of some distinction.

During this period, *waka*—31-syllable poems in 5-7-5-7-7 form—became popular among the court ladies, nobles and priests. In 905 A.D., the *Kokinshu* was compiled as the first anthology of poems collected under an Imperial order.

The rise of the warriors as the ruling class led to a period of about 150 years from the end of the 12th century when tales of war became popular.

The following two centuries produced a number of major works in which the soldier replaces the courtier as hero. Two of the outstanding ones are *Heike Monogatari* (The Tale of Heike), around 1233, and *Taiheiki* (A Chronicle of Medieval Japan), appearing in the mid-1300's.

The 16th century was a period of civil war and hardly any literature was produced, but a great literary revival began in the latter part of the 17th century. The novels of Saikaku Ihara (1642-93) and the plays of Monzaemon Chikamatsu (1653-1724) were written for a wider audience which included the newly risen merchant class and were of very high literary merit.

About this time *haiku* emerged as a new form of verse, its greatest exponent being Basho (1644-94).

Western literature swept into Japan during the 19th century like a wave, sometimes invigorating and sometimes confusing. A hectic period of literary experimentation and development followed.

Japanese literature was enriched by the different currents of Western thought, such

Yasunari Kawabata, winner of the Nobel Prize for Literature in 1969 (above).
Interior of a well-stocked bookstore in Tokyo (below). ▶

as liberalism, idealism and romanticism. Japanese writers turned their hand to Western-style novels, and the different trends and currents of thought derived from the West flourished side by side.

Outstanding novelists such as Ogai Mori and Soseki Natsume produced their works at the turn of the century. These are still widely read today.

Western literary works are translated in great number into Japanese, and the great names of the West, from Shakespeare, Goethe and Tolstoy to contemporary masters of literature, are perhaps as familiar in Japan as in their own countries.

Despite the impact of Western literature, traditional Japanese forms still flourish. *Waka* and *haiku*, for instance, are penned today by a huge number of poets, both professional and amateur, with all the skill and enthusiasm of the court aristocrats of the past.

Since the war, a growing number of Japanese works have been introduced abroad. English translations of contemporary works that have been widely read include "Homecoming" by Jiro Osaragi, "The Sound of Waves" and other novels by Yukio Mishima, and "Some Prefer Nettles" by Junichiro Tanizaki. Arthur Waley's "The Tale of Genji" and other translations of Japanese classics are also widely read.

In 1968, Yasunari Kawabata was awarded the Nobel Prize for Literature. He is the first Japanese ever to receive the coveted prize in the field of literature.

Kawabata is widely known abroad through his works translated into foreign languages, such as "*Yukiguni*" (Snow Country), "*Senbazuru*" (A Thousand Cranes) and "*Koto*" (Kyoto).

His style of writing is marked by the pursuit of the beauty of Japanese lyricism with a sharpened sensibility. His works are said to have inherited the esthetic consciousness of Japan's ancient dynastic literature with a touch of incisiveness.

ART

Japanese art is as diverse today as its tra-

◄Garden of the Samboin Temple, Kyoto.

ditions are long with a past rich in achievement and a present alive with enthusiastic creative endeavors.

The oldest surviving objects of Japanese art are earthen images dating from the Stone Age and crude stone figures of a somewhat later period. A yet later development were mortuary clay images called *haniwa*, which have been excavated from ancient mausolea. These show some technical advance and are highly prized today as examples of primitive art.

The introduction of Buddhism in 538 A.D. led to a period of sudden artistic flowering that reached its height in the Asuka Period (538-646), when the arts were encouraged under Imperial patronage. Many Buddhist temples were built, including the celebrated Horyuji Temple, near Nara, which is believed to be the oldest wooden building in the world.

The Buddhist influence is particularly evident in sculpture, which flourished in this period. The emphasis was on solemnity and sublimity, and features were idealized.

The Hakuho Period (646-710), which followed the Asuka Period, was a time of strong Chinese and Indian influence. The flatness of form and stiffness of expression in the sculpture of the Asuka Period were replaced by grace and vigor.

The Tempyo Period (710-784) was the golden age of Buddhism and Buddhist sculpture in Japan. Some of the great works of this period may be seen in and around Nara today. They reflect a great realism, which is combined with a rare serenity.

An idealized style of expression returned in the following Jogan Period (784-899), when the mystical teachings of the esoteric Mikkyo Buddhist sect influenced the sculpture of the time. The statues of this period are massive in form and mystic in expression.

The Jogan Period marked the first 100 years of the Heian Period, which continued until 1192. The Fujiwara family held sway, and the characteristics of the sculpture of this period are elegance and beauty, sometimes at the expense of strength.

Contact with China had been broken and the influences previously introduced from abroad were now assimilated to evolve a new type of Japanese art. Delicacy and exquisiteness of form mark the new artistic taste that evolved at that time. These characteristics are also seen in the unique architecture of the period. The most beautiful example of the harmony of tone of Heian architecture is the Ho-o-do (Phoenix Hall) of the Byodoin monastery near Kyoto.

Painting assumed an important position during this period, almost for the first time. It was in this era that the type of painting known as *Yamatoe* and the art of *Emakimono* (illustrated scrolls) developed.

The austerity of the warrior-class regime and of Zen Buddhism was reflected in the subsequent Kamakura Period (1192-1333), when sculpture became extremely realistic in style and vigorous in expression. The Zen influence was reflected in the purity and simplicity of the architecture of the period. Traces of the influence of the tradition established in the Kamakura Period can be found in Japanese architecture even today. Illustrated scrolls and portrait painting were also in vogue during this period.

Sumie, the delicate style of brush painting with black ink, was developed in the Muromachi Period (1333-1573). It originated with the Buddhists of the Zen sect who were familiar with the art of the Chinese Ming Dynasty.

The Azuchi-Momoyama Period (1573-1603), which followed, was a time of transition. It was also a period of great artistic sophistication. Artists expressed themselves in bright colors and elaborate designs. Gorgeous folding screens were introduced. Castles and temples were decorated with elaborate wood carvings. Masks of great artistic refinement began to be worn in the Noh dramas.

The most famous single artistic form in the Tokugawa Period (1603-1867) is perhaps the *ukiyoe* genre print, which won immense popularity among the general public. The influence of *ukiyoe* on European art in the latter half of the 19th century is well known. Sculpture declined during the Tokugawa Period, but considerable advances were made in handicrafts.

A special mention must be made in any review of Japanese fine arts of the Katsura Detached Palace in Kyoto. It was built in the early Tokugawa Period and is famous for its superb harmony and rare simplicity. The garden is considered one of the finest examples of Japanese landscape gardening.

The second half of the 19th century was a period when Western influences made themselves felt on Japanese art. Today, Western forms and traditional Japanese styles exist side by side and sometimes mingle with each other in a new process of mutual assimilation and reinvigoration.

The Japanese show a deep interest in artistic developments, both as spectators and as practitioners. Painting and drawing are unusually popular spare-time pursuits. A large number of art exhibitions are held at all times of the year in the main cities and draw large crowds. Japan's oldest and most impressive annual art show is the comprehensive Nitten Art Exhibition; to be selected for display in the Nitten is one of the nation's highest art honors.

Since the war there has been a brisk international artistic exchange. Many Japanese paintings and other works of art have been shown abroad and numerous exhibitions of foreign works are held in Japan.

The Japan International Art Exhibition, which is also called "Tokyo Biennale," is now included among the four largest art exhibitions in the world.

The International Biennial Exhibition of Prints, held in Tokyo and Kyoto, is world famous in the field of prints.

The Japanese love of art and nature is reflected in many aspects of their daily lives, in their architecture and in the popularity of flower arrangement and the tea ceremony.

MUSIC

The works of the orchestral repertoire of the West are as much a part of Japan's musical life as the traditional music played on *shamisen*, *shakuhachi*, or *koto*. Modern jazz is today as popular as the traditional ballads of ancient Japan.

One of the oldest forms of Japanese music, still preserved at the Imperial Court and at some Shinto shrines, is *Gagaku*

Ho-o-do (Phoenix Hall) of Byodoin Temple, Kyoto, built in 1053 (above).
Katsura Imperial Villa, Kyoto, completed in 1624 (below).▶

(Court music and dance). This derives from a style of music introduced to Japan in the eighth century from China of the T'ang Dynasty which had earlier absorbed the ancient music of Persia, India, and Korea. It is highly stylized and evokes the elaborate rituals of a bygone age. *Gagaku* is publicly performed in Japan from time to time, and the Court musicians have given performances abroad on two occasions: in 1959 in the United States and in 1970 in Europe.

Instrumental music can be represented by three typical instruments: the *shamisen*, a balalaika-type instrument of three strings; the *shakuhachi*, a clarinet-like instrument made of several joints of a bamboo stem; and the *koto*, a low, long instrument with 13 silk strings. The *shamisen* is played as accompaniment for Kabuki and Bunraku and for "Buyo" (classical dancing). The *shakuhachi*, formerly restricted to priests of a Zen sect of Buddhism prior to the Meiji Restoration, has developed a rather large following of foreign musicians who find a fascination in the grandeur of its sound and the profundity of its timbre. The *koto*, perhaps the most popular and widely played Japanese instrument, is primarily used in solo performance, as accompaniment for "Buyo," or in massed recitals.

Western music began to develop alongside Japanese music in the latter half of the 19th century. It has been taught in schools from the elementary grade since the 1870's.

Every conceivable form of Western music is performed, composed and enjoyed in Japan today. Tokyo has six permanent symphony orchestras, and there are other orchestras in the Kansai district. There are seven musical conservatories in Tokyo, turning out a stream of new performers and vocalists, as well as numerous dancing academies where ballet is taught. Concerts, recitals and performances of opera and ballet draw large audiences with programs of works by composers ranging from Bach to the most modern experimentalists. Musical talent is encouraged and sought out by national music contests that are held several times a year.

Every year there is a steady flow of celebrated foreign musicians and organizations coming to perform in Japan. The list of foreign orchestras, soloists, conductors, ballet and opera troupes who have visited Japan in recent years reads like a directory of the world's leading artistic talent.

Each spring, many of the world's most famous musicians and ensembles travel to Japan to take part in the Osaka International Festival, the only event of its kind in Asia. The Festival, inaugurated in 1958, aims to promote international cultural exchange and to encourage the training and development of individual artistic talent.

The 1970 Osaka Festival, held in conjunction with the 1970 Japan World Exposition in Osaka, consisted of a total of 83 performances under 30 different programs, encompassing operas, orchestral performances, chamber music ensembles, ballet programs, recitals and stage dramas.

Japanese musicians themselves are performing overseas more frequently than ever before and are achieving a growing international reputation. Three orchestras, namely the NHK (Japan Broadcasting Corporation) Symphony Orchestra, the Yomiuri Nippon Philharmonic, and the Japan Philharmonic have made a number of successful tours of Europe, the United States, Latin America and Southeast Asia. Individual conductors are also drawing attention abroad, with Seiji Ozawa the most prominent as the former musical director of the Toronto (Canada) Symphony and more recently elected as conductor of the San Francisco Symphony in the United States.

The preservation as well as development of Japanese music in its classical forms is not being neglected. One group dedicated to cultivating new Japanese music within its classical tradition is the Ensemble Nipponia, formed in 1964 and consisting of distinguished soloists and composers. While a chamber orchestra complete with Japanese wind, string and percussion instruments, it has a broad repertoire using all or some of the instruments or at times a single instrument in solo performance, in forms approaching the Western style of composition.

◄ *The Ensemble Nipponia in concert performance (above).*
The NHK Symphony Orchestra at Tokyo's Metropolitan Festival Hall (below).

THEATER

The theatrical arts flourish in Japan with a vigor that has carried their fame across the world. They are perhaps unique in their variety, ranging from the formal stateliness of Noh drama to the down-to-earth lustiness of popular vaudeville, from puppet drama whose traditions have been handed down through the centuries to elaborate wide-screen productions of one of the most prolific cinema industries in the world.

The three major forms of classical Japanese drama are Noh, Bunraku (puppet dramas) and Kabuki. The oldest of these is Noh, which traces its origins back to the 13th century, when various rituals and religious dances of the preceding eras were integrated and developed. Noh reached its present form in the early 15th century.

It is a highly stylized dramatic form and was originally performed exclusively for the upper classes. The classic traditions are kept alive today by performers, many of whom come from a hereditary line of Noh artists. Noh now has a relatively limited following, but its profound dignity, eloquent symbolism and classic grace will always command the enthusiastic admiration of its devotees.

A growing number of foreigners are joining the ranks of admirers of the Noh dance and drama. Noh was performed at the International Drama Festival in Venice in 1954. It has also been presented in Europe, the United States and Mexico.

The Bunraku puppet drama dates back to the 16th century and developed to its present form in the 18th century. It is performed regularly at the Bunraku-za theater in Osaka and is seen periodically in Tokyo. The puppets are elaborate, half life-size dolls whose movements are controlled by up to three puppeteers. They perform their dramas to the accompaniment of *shamisen* music and narration and create a powerful illusion of human emotion and feeling. It is a highly developed artistic form, quite of its own kind. Interest abroad in Bunraku has been steadily developing and the first Bunraku troupe to perform outside Japan toured the United States in the spring of 1966. It was also presented in Europe in 1968.

Kabuki, Japan's most famous dramatic form, derives from both Noh and Bunraku, as well as incorporating other theatrical arts from an earlier age. It developed into its present form in the late 17th century. In its earliest days, it was performed by a troupe of women and later by young males, but since it crystallized into its present form, it has been performed exclusively by men.

Kabuki faithfully preserves the rich traditions of its distinguished past. Many of its most famous plays have delighted audiences for more than two centuries with little change. The Kabuki repertoire, however, also contains a large number of new plays written by contemporary authors. In recent years, some moves have also been made to modernize Kabuki and a number of productions have been staged in which some modifications have been made in the style of presentation.

This dramatic art also enjoys an international reputation and four grand tours have already been made abroad: to New York and San Francisco in 1960, to Moscow in 1961, to Berlin, Paris and Lisbon in 1965 and again to the United States in 1969.

As well as its rich classical dramatic heritage, the Japanese theater also offers modern drama in the Western style. Serving as a bridge between the two is a group called *Shimpa*, which was founded toward the end of the 19th century. *Shimpa* has its roots in the Kabuki tradition—originally, for instance, it was performed only by male actors—but it is now a distinct form of its own with a natural style of acting. The action is usually set among the common people, and the cast includes actresses as well as actors.

Drama in the Western style is presented by a number of theatrical troupes. These first appeared about 60 years ago and today command a considerable following, especially among younger people. Their repertoire is extremely wide, ranging from the classics of such masters as Shakespeare, Moliere, Ibsen and Chekhov to modern plays by contemporary playwrights, both Japanese and foreign.

Japan's three classic stage arts: Noh (above left); Bunraku (above right); and Kabuki (below) ▶

The most vigorous dramatic form in Japan today is still the motion picture. The first Japanese motion picture was made about half a century ago. In contrast to the rising popularity of television programs, however, the movie industry is on the decline. The number of movie theaters declined from 7,457 in 1960 to 3,602 in December 1969. Attendance also declined from 1,014 million in 1960 to 287 million in 1969.

Japan's film studios are among the most productive in the world, turning out 494 feature films in 1968, of which 260 were color and 475 widescreen productions. Short subject production is also at a high level, amounting to a total of 1,286 films in 1968 with more than 80 per cent in color.

Japanese films have received numerous awards for technical and artistic excellence in various international film festivals. "Rashomon" was the first Japanese production to be awarded a Grand Prix, receiving it at the 1951 Venice Film Festival. Other Grand Prix winners include "Gate of Hell" (1954), "The Rickshaw Man" (1958), "The Island" (1961), "Fires on the Plain" (1961), "Classroom Renegades" (1963 Moscow) and "Bushido—A Samurai Saga" (1963 Berlin).

There are also films which received other international prizes: "Woman in the Dunes" (1964), "Kwaidan" (1965) and "The Great White Tower" (1967).

In 1969, Japan exported 2,587 films, of which 2,144 were features, 45 were short subjects and 398 were newsreels.

In the same year, 253 foreign films, including 121 American, 41 Italian, 27 French and 23 British, were released in Japan.

RELIGION

Freedom of religion is guaranteed to all under the Constitution of 1946, which states:
"No religious organization shall receive any privileges from the State, nor exercise any political authority. No person shall be compelled to take part in any religious act, celebration, rites or practice. The State and its organs shall refrain from religious education or any other religious activity."

Buddhism is the major religion in Japan and has a following of 83,290,000. Christianity is also active, and there are estimated to be more than 830,000 Christians in Japan.

Shintoism which cannot be regarded as a religion in the strict sense of the word is Japan's indigenous cult and is concerned with the worship of the Imperial ancestors and the family ancestors. During World War II it was regarded as a State religion and encouraged by the authorities. Under the Constitution, it no longer receives any special official encouragement or privileges.

Shintoism exists side by side and sometimes overlaps in the popular mind with Buddhism. Many Japanese today go through Shinto rites when they marry, and when they die, Buddhist funeral rites are performed.

Buddhism was introduced to Japan from India through China and Korea around the middle of the 6th century. It not only flourished as a religion but did much to enrich the country's arts and learning.

Christianity was brought to Japan in 1549 by the Jesuit missionary, St. Francis Xavier. It spread rapidly in the second half of the century. It was later proscribed and remained banned for about 250 years until the middle of the 19th century, when Japan re-opened its doors to the rest of the world.

Protestants slightly outnumber Catholics among the Christians in Japan today. The Protestants in 1959 celebrated the centenary of their arrival in Japan.

Confucianism is a code of moral precepts rather than a religion. It was introduced into Japan at the beginning of the 6th century and has had a great influence on Japanese thought and behavior. Its influence has somewhat declined since the war.

◄ *Miroku Bosatsu, wooden statue of a meditating Bodhisattva, carved in the early part of the 7th century (above).*
Inner Shrine of the Grand Shrines of Ise, fountainhead of the Shinto faith (below).

SPORTS

In 1964, Tokyo was the host city for the 18th Olympic Games. When the world's top athletes came to Japan for that event, they found themselves in a country where almost every single Western sport is played, in addition to the traditional Japanese sports such as Sumo (Japanese wrestling), Judo, Kendo (Japanese fencing) and Kyudo (Japanese archery).

They also found themselves in a country with an established tradition of major sports meetings. In 1958, the Third Asian Games were successfully held in Tokyo and in 1967, the Universiade was also held in Tokyo. An even bigger meeting, in terms of the numbers of athletes participating, is held every year. This is the National Sports Festival, an amateur event that features almost every type of athletics. More than 16,000 young athletes from all over Japan take part in this Festival.

Every type of sport, both traditional and modern, has a huge following in Japan. Sports newspapers and magazines are avidly read. Crowds pack the sports stadiums for all major athletic events, while millions more follow their favorite sports on television.

Radio and television have greatly revived the popularity across the country of Sumo, Japan's traditional style of wrestling. The beginnings of Sumo are lost in the mists of antiquity, but it goes back in legend more than 2,000 years. It is a highly formalized but dramatic sport, closely followed today by almost every Japanese. Six regular Sumo tournaments, each lasting 15 days, are held every year in Tokyo and other big cities. Professional Sumo wrestlers spend the rest of the year touring the provinces.

Judo, developed from the old art known as *jujutsu*, is today a popular sport not only in Japan but in many other countries. It was included for the first time in the Olympic Games in 1964. The first international Judo championships were held in Tokyo in 1956. International championships are now held at regular intervals, not only in Japan but overseas. At home, the annual All-Japan Judo Tournament attracts keen interest all over the country.

Kendo waned in popularity after the war but is now enjoying a revival.

In addition to their traditional sports, the Japanese engage in almost every form of Western athletics, from track and field events to baseball, soccer, rugby, swimming, rowing and equestrianism.

Many Japanese athletes have taken part in international sports meetings overseas, including the Olympic Games, and numerous foreign teams and individual athletes have been invited to Japan both before and since the war.

Baseball is one of the most popular sports in Japan today. It has been described as the national sport and is played both as an amateur and as a professional game, but whether the competing teams are school children playing on a sand lot or rival professional league leaders, any game can be sure of attracting a large crowd of eager spectators.

Golf is also establishing itself as a popular sport in Japan. There are approximately 560 courses in Japan today and about 3.5 million golfers.

Skiing and skating are the two most popular winter sports in Japan, stimulated by the ideal winter climate and the many suitable mountain sites and resorts. It is estimated that Japan has more than six million skiers and skaters each, with the figure increasing steadily each year.

The combination of ideal weather and numerous mountain ranges has also aroused an enthusiasm for mountain climbing. Aside from hundreds of groups climbing the Japan Alps at home, Japanese teams are active scaling peaks abroad. In May 1970, a Japanese team became the sixth in the world to reach the summit of Mt. Everest.

Japanese sportsmen have also established their mark in international contests in volley ball, table tennis, amateur wrestling and gymnastics. More than 200 Japanese athletes took part in the 19th Olympic Games in Mexico in 1968 and won 25 medals in all (11 gold, 7 silver and 7 bronze). Japanese sportsmen ranked third after the United States and the Soviet Union in the number of gold medals acquired.

A second international athletic honor has been awarded Japan. In April 1966, the International Olympic Committee (IOC) designated Sapporo, the capital city of Hokkaido, Japan's northern islands, as the site of the 1972 Winter Olympic Games.

Traditional sports of Japan: Sumo (above left), Judo (above right), and Kendo (below).▶